THE PASSION
FOR LIBERTY

THE PASSION
FOR LIBERTY

TIBOR R. MACHAN

ROWMAN & LITTLEFIELD PUBLISHERS, INC.
Lanham • Boulder • New York • Oxford

ROWMAN & LITTLEFIELD PUBLISHERS, INC.

Published in the United States of America
by Rowman & Littlefield Publishers, Inc.
A Member of the Rowman & Littlefield Publishing Group
4501 Forbes Boulevard, Suite 200, Lanham, Maryland 20706
www.rowmanlittlefield.com

PO Box 317
Oxford
OX2 9RU, UK

British Library Cataloging in Publication Information Available

Library of Congress Cataloging-in-Publication Data
Machan, Tibor R.
  The passion for liberty / Tibor R. Machan.
    p. cm.
Includes bibliographical references and index.
  ISBN 0-7425-3102-3 (alk. paper) — ISBN 0-7425-3103-1 (pbk.: alk.
paper)
  1. Liberty. 2. Civil Rights—United States. 3. Democracy—United
States. I. Title.
  JC599.U5 M263 2003
  320'.01'1—dc21

                                                          2002152681

Printed in the United States of America

♾™ The paper used in this publication meets the minimum requirements of
American National Standard for Information Sciences—Permanence of Paper
for Printed Library Materials, ANSI/NISO Z39.48-1992.

This book is dedicated to the memory of Ernest van Den Haag, a mentor, friend, and formidable intellectual adversary.

CONTENTS

PREFACE

When I was a boy in Budapest, Hungary, I learned about the meaning of human freedom and how a bad political regime can squash it nearly completely. Later, after I was smuggled out from that communist hellhole, sadly I experienced another kind of oppression at the hands of my father, a virulent Nazi sympathizer and a brutal parent. Although these early experiences didn't give me all the right answers about freedom, I have never let go of the conviction that freedom has enormous significance for human beings. My personal experiences sparked and still sustain my tireless interest in the meaning of human liberty.

Since that time I have had the good fortune not to rely solely on my own experiences but also to embark on an academic study of political life, its numerous twists and turns, the different conceptions people have developed about how we should live together in our communities. My passion for liberty may have given me a good emotional grounding for keeping alive my interest, but it would not have sufficed for purposes of gaining a good understanding of all the relevant elements of human liberty. After all, feeling badly about how a regime treats those who are subject to its rule is not reliable—one can easily misplace passion and let it misguide one's focus. So it is important to take up the serious study of alternative political systems, to learn why the various ways that people conceive of a just political order are appealing, and to learn their strengths and weaknesses.

That is why I took up the discipline of political philosophy: so as not to remain captive of my personal history.

Over the years I have thought and written much about the foundations of freedom and why so many find it unsatisfactory to rely on the institutions that sustain it. In the following pages, I lay out most of my reasons for having remained loyal to the idea that the most important element of an organized human community is a constitution that identifies and aims to protect the principles of individual liberty. In the following pages I defend, in what might best be called layman's terms, a libertarian conception of the free society: that is, a society in which "negative rights"—rights not to be interfered with in one's peaceful pursuits—are identified and protected.

Why is such a society best for human inhabitation? Can the idea that individual liberty is most vital for human beings be applied wherever human beings live—or is this merely true only for some people? What about objections, such as that a truly free society would lead to the unjust neglect of poor or helpless persons, foster immorality, and lead to the neglect of higher goods, spirituality, and the like?

I discuss these and numerous related details in terms that can be grasped by any reasonably interested and educated reader. Some questions that people pose to champions of human liberty need special treatment. Thus I deal with the claims of those who propose that democracy trumps individual rights. I explore the conflict between consequentialist and rights-based approaches to political issues. I also deal with the relationship between foreign policy and democracy and with the even more particular questions of affirmative action, abortion, military intervention, whether torture is ever justified in a world of terrorism, and so forth.

It is one thing to understand that what human beings require most in their communities is that others treat them as adults, not as children whose lives must often be forcibly guided by their elder and wiser guardians. It is another thing to also feel through one's bones that a free society is a good society, as good as it can get when it comes to laying out the principles by which members of communities should be expected to deal with one another. Of course, there is so much else that people need beside sound political ideas and ideals so as to make the most of their lives: How to raise children properly, how to be productive, creative, generous, kind, and prudent—all these are matters everyone must address. In their communities, however, the requirement that everyone's right to liberty be taken very seriously, indeed, is primary. I wish, of course, to lay out the reasons for this, yet I want also to indicate why it is important to be passionately loyal to those requirements.

ACKNOWLEDGMENTS

I wish to express my heartfelt appreciation to all those who have discussed with me my work over the last several years. J. Roger Lee, Jim Chesher, Nathaniel Branden, Aeon Skoble, and Randall Dipert have helped me explore my topic. I want to thank John Raisian of the Hoover Institution for his support of my work. Others, such as Dave Threshie, chairman of the board of directors of Freedom Communications, Inc.; Sam Wolgemuth, past-president and CEO of Freedom Communications, Inc.; and Homa Shabahang of the University of San Francisco, have also been very supportive. The editorial assistance of David M. Brown is much appreciated, having made this work much more accessible than it otherwise would be.

Some of the work in this book is reworked from essays that have been published previously and I wish to thank the publishers for their permission to make use of them.

These include *Commentaries on Law & Public Policy* (The Dumont Institute); *Hoover Essays in Public Policy*, Hoover Institution Press; *The Journal of Value Inquiry*; *Modern Age, Journal of Social Philosophy*; *Ideas on Liberty*; *The Occasional Review*; and *The Journal of Libertarian Studies*.

I thank the Hoover Institution, Chapman University's Leatherby Center and Freedom Communications, Inc., for their financial help with my preparation of this book for publication. Special thanks are due to John Raisian, Sam Wolgemuth, Dave Threshie, and Jim Doti for their ongoing encouragement of my work. I also wish to thank Nancy Gregory for her assistance.

INTRODUCTION: FOR INDIVIDUAL RIGHTS

We hold these truths to be self-evident, that all Men are created equal, that they are endowed by their Creator with certain unalienable Rights, that among these are Life, Liberty, and the pursuit of Happiness—That to secure these rights, Governments are instituted among Men, deriving their just powers from the consent of the governed, that whenever any Form of Government becomes destructive of these ends, it is the Right of the People to alter or to abolish it, and to institute new Government, laying its foundation on such principles, and organizing its powers in such form, as to them shall seem most likely to effect their Safety and Happiness.

—Thomas Jefferson,
The Declaration of Independence

The founding of the United States of America represented a major political revolution.

Some conservatives dispute this, yet the break with the past was far greater than any before or since. The Marxist-Leninist upheaval in Russia in 1917 was minor in comparison. The great Russian Revolution was in essence a *putsch,* a change of despots, from czar to communist-fascist dictator—a disaster for the Russian people, to be sure, but essentially just more of what had gone on before.

The American founding, by contrast, for the first time officially declared the principles of a vitally different approach to how government is to relate to the people—as *citizens,* not as *subjects.*

Both before and after America's "discovery," the nations of the world have been ruled by one or another collectivist ideal, more or less brutally. America's founders articulated the view that every individual human being is sovereign. None is to be governed without his or her consent. The rights to life, liberty, and the pursuit of happiness are nothing other than prohibitions against intruding on the individual against his or her consent.[1]

The individualist view of the founders still resonates somewhat in the United States—but just barely. The discovery of rights has fashioned many American institutions, from criminal law to the capitalist economic system, but the influence of the original American political ideas has been so weakened that, by now, little is left of the early respect for individual rights.[2]

Today we supposedly no longer have rights to life, liberty, and the pursuit of happiness but only to guaranteed provisions from others: minimum wages, unemployment compensation, medical care, a risk-free environment, job security, security in old age, and—as one New York City public service ad announced—not to be lonely! So the right to life—meaning that we have the right to act peacefully to further our lives and that no one may kill us with impunity—has metamorphosed into the right to all the benefits that we might possibly obtain in life. We are presumably entitled to obtain these benefits whether or not we exert the necessary effort ourselves, whether or not others are willing to help us when we need help.[3] In other words, the mere existence of an individual's stipulated need subjects others to involuntary servitude.

In this way the American revolution has been nearly voided! The explicit prohibition against the violation of one's right to life, liberty, and the pursuit of happiness—the prohibition against involuntary servitude—has been rescinded, and consent is now superfluous. So doctors are forced to deliver services on the terms set by the government; insurance companies must serve on command, not by consent; and businesses must employ workers on terms set by the state. Indeed, under the guise of individual rights, all the original rights that delimit and protect our individual sovereignty have been eroded.

What has happened to the freest country in the world?[4] Is it in regression? Before we can answer, we need to make a detour. We need to examine the case for the kinds of rights that at least originally distinguished the American polity.

ASSUMPTIONS OF NATURAL RIGHTS THEORY

The American polity was established under the strong influence of natural rights theory. This theory is an approach to answering the question: How, in the most general terms, should human beings live with each other? It begins with an investigation of human nature itself so as to arrive at the most basic and general answer. (How we should answer political questions is a vital issue of political philosophy, the field that investigates the basic principles of human community life.)

Political theory draws upon virtually all other fields of philosophical and social inquiry. It considers all sorts of factors about human beings and their relationships, environment, sustenance, goals, and purposes. It aims to grasp the *oughts* or *musts* of a just human community—its proper organizing principles.

To make some headway here, first we need to explore the more personal realm of ethics or natural law. We need to consider whether it is even possible to speak of what individuals morally should do in their lives. Then we need to consider public or political organization—what is the just framework for human community life?

If by "rights" we mean social devices *invented* by us as a kind of rootless and arbitrary convention, they could be in total flux. Conventional "rights" are unlimited by any guiding principle exclusive of the sheer demands of those who claim them—not even the principle that they ought not clash with other such "rights." Thus they can be as many and various as anyone may desire. Such an approach to rights will not provide stable or objective principles for social organization. Under such a regime the powerful will rule—by virtue of their power, not by virtue of the clarity and truth of ideas that can justify particular social conduct. Nor will others have a means to curb that power based on what is really right and wrong. When the fulfillment of *any* kind of claim on others is seen as justified as long as it is formulated in terms of conventional "rights," to that extent any standards of actual and objective right and wrong are banned from political discourse.

But if it is indeed possible for us to investigate reality and human nature, we can ground rights objectively and steer clear of such indiscriminate usage. Contrary to the skeptics, we can indeed obtain such knowledge. For insofar as we admit that we can make sense of even the minimum of our lives, we thereby affirm that reality hangs together in a reasonably orderly fashion, at least at the most basic level; and this must be true also of such essential realms as ethics and politics.[5] The inhabitants of the world, both animate and inanimate, have specific natures or identities. They act in certain ways that are consistent with those identities. If we can grant at least that we can identify something about the world, then we concede thereby that knowledge (correct awareness or identification of the world) is possible in principle.

It remains then to discover what are the appropriate principles of identification for any particular area of inquiry. How we obtain knowledge depends on what sort of knowledge we are seeking—what aspect of the world is under investigation. If we want to find out about the past, memory and records of that memory give us knowledge; in biology, experimentation with members of the same species of living beings, and our awareness of the behavior and makeup of the members of this species as compared with those of other species, will provide us with knowledge; and in sociology, we gain knowledge through the careful observation of how groups of people behave and the interpretation of this observation in light of what we already know about human nature and society. The fact that different methods of inquiry are appropriate to different fields is important because sometimes it is thought that, unless the standards of knowledge in any field abide by the standards of knowledge in one, it is impossible to have knowledge in the former.[6] This, however, would imply that every aspect of reality must be equivalent to every other aspect—a kind of reductionism that reconstructs the world based on methodological assumptions rather than on grounding those assumptions in the world as it actually is, with all its features and relations. (Some aspects of method are indeed universal; the most basic requirements of logic and evidence would apply to every field, for instance.)

Once we have gotten a glimpse of human nature, we can then ask how considerations of "ought" apply in the case of human beings as such. That, in turn, will provide us with the basic material needed to determine the "oughts" of interpersonal conduct and of political life.[7]

So let us consider now how norms can arise at all in nature.

KNOWLEDGE OF VALUES

We are familiar enough with certain facts concerning inanimate and animate existence—rocks are hard, dogs often bark, penicillin can prevent disease, governments often wage war. These kinds of facts can be known without much debate about them. But very soon after we admit that we know something along these lines, we find that other matters we think we know are extremely controversial.

That Napoleon should have prepared his men better for the Battle of Waterloo, or that Teddy Roosevelt should not have led the U.S. into war, or that the president should fight against inflation by refusing to print more money, or that one should respect the wishes of one's mate when considering where to choose one's next home—all these are facts or alleged facts about which much controversy arises. But the sheer fact of controversy does not tell us about the state of our knowledge of a controversial claim; it only tells us that at least one of those who contradicts the other about a conclusion must be wrong. Controversy is a social problem that anyone who wishes to tell others what he knows (or claims to know) will encounter. To understand this better, first we need to find out whether there is anything we do know about controversial topics.

Natural rights theory answers this question by noting, first, that considerations of what one should do depend upon considerations of what is good and evil. That which is good (and possible) for one to pursue is something one ought to pursue, and that which is bad (and possible) for one to pursue one ought not to pursue.

But how do we come to know what is good? Here we need to consider what "good" means insofar as it characterizes an entity or organism. It means the fullest realization of some particular thing as an instance of its kind. For example, a good peach is a fully realized peach, or a peach that has most fully attained the nature of being a peach by being robust rather than stunted or shriveled. A good tennis game is a fully realized tennis game, or a tennis game that has fully reached the crux of a tennis game: for instance, one in which the players are somewhat evenly matched and the ball at least sometimes crosses the net.

Whenever we appraise tomatoes, peaches, apples, chickens, or whatever, we can learn that we should praise it or criticize it by reference to the fact that the thing (or activity or whatnot) in question has more or less fully reached its distinctive nature in the given case at hand. The nature of something— what it is that makes it the kind of thing it is (e.g., a tennis game, a golf ball, or a Christmas tree)—is the place or category it occupies in the most rational, or factually based, way of classifying existence (e.g., trees, chairs, furniture, balloons, time, days, weeks, months, space, field, meadow, galaxy, mind, memory, imagination, or an idea).[8] A tennis game is a good one if the players play by satisfying the central ingredients of tennis and whatever those ingredients imply for the particular game at hand, which may require realizing the game somewhat differently from another particular game. A good skiing slope, a good knife, or a good source of light—all these pertain to how fully some particular case realizes the essence of what it is in its own instance. We don't always talk of a good this or a good that, or a bad this or a bad that, but such expressions as "great," "neat," "swell," "far out," "groovy," and "fantastic" make the same point for us, as do ones such as "lousy," "rotten," and "poor." Most generally, when we consider what good is, it has to do with whether something has realized its nature in the instance at hand.

HUMAN NATURE

In the case of human beings, the consideration of what is good leads to the issue of the relationship between human actions and being good. Being a good human being, like being a good anything, requires the fullest possible realization of one's nature in one's particular case—or at least that one's actions in a particular instance are consistent with the realization of one's nature rather than antagonistic to and destructive of it. So, knowledge of human nature will enable us to tell how to be good at being human—how to survive and flourish qua *human* being as opposed to some other kind of living thing.

This is where the naturalism of natural rights theory comes into full focus. Natural rights theory can produce an understanding of the rights that human beings have by reference to an understanding of human nature. That is why they are called *natural* rights—they are rights that someone has or that we are justified to ascribe to someone by virtue of his or her human nature! Human nature pertains to what is true of human beings just insofar as they are human beings and not anything else (e.g., not as students, mothers, Germans, or twenty-five-year-olds, or as squirrels, inanimate objects, or geometrical figures). What then is a human being as such? What is human nature?

Human beings are animals with a biological nature and all that involves; they are the kind of animal capable of rational thought (i.e., able to think in terms of principles, ideas, or concepts). The ancient idea that man is a rational animal is still sound, although exactly what the idea means has had to be modified in light of our greater understanding of the issues involved. Still, the crucial point is that human beings are by nature animals who are capable of rationality and choice. A good human being would thus be one who, speaking very generally indeed, acts rationally with regard to her own life. (Of course, what "acting rationally" means in detail for one's particular life may differ in important respects from what it means for another's particular life.) This does not yet tell us all about what constitutes morally good conduct, but it is an indispensable start.[9]

ETHICS

The first normative area of concern is personal ethics—in other words, the code or laws of nature that pertain to how we should conduct ourselves. By nature we live a most fully human life by being rational. We thus achieve the highest level of well-being available to us on all possible levels—to the extent that a specific aspect of our life is subject to our control.

To the best of our knowledge, the bulk of the animate world behaves as if guided automatically—by instincts, drives, reflexes, and so forth. Human beings, however, are not compelled or directed by such automatic drives to behave as they do. Rather, they are able to choose between genuine alternatives. Maybe, in a more limited way than we do, some animals can, too. Human beings may also have some instincts, but if this is the case, this fact is negligible or borderline. The point is that people in maturity are indeed able to choose what they will do. (We are not discussing childhood or even adolescence, although a fuller discussion would have to consider those stages as well.)

The fact that human beings enjoy the freedom that other animals lack in the area of thinking is central. To live, even to the minimum degree of viability, a solitary adult needs to figure things out; only then can he take the actions that his life requires for sustenance. He can choose of course to wither away and die, in which case thinking is not required of him. But we are not concerned with those human beings who do not choose to live and thus have no interest in the principles of human conduct and of human living! Ethical norms are relevant to us because we lack innate drives or prepro- grammed instructions to guide us in living, but if we will not live, those norms are beside the point.[10] The normal case, of course, is not only that we do choose to live but also that we are naturally inclined to do so. Suicide is not generally the re- sult of offhand philosophical deliberation but of deep despair or hopelessness for a life gone wrong. Moral guidance may well provide the means of making such a life again appear vi- able.

The first point, then, about moral norms is that they are re- quired only for those whose lives are under their own gover- nance and within their realm of choice. From the fact that our capacity for thought needs to be initiated or put into effect by us, we learn that the human good is indeed, at a crucial level, a matter of personal initiative—of choice.

THE PRIMACY OF THINKING

If we don't do our own thinking, we merely coast or float about—usually on the opinions of others—based on accident and mere osmosis. Living requires, among other things, firsthand thought, rational observation, reflection, consideration, recollec- tion, assessment, evaluation, and comparison. That doesn't mean we can't learn from others, but we still have to use our minds to evaluate what we are taught, the credibility of authorities, and so forth. Natural rights theory relies upon this natural fact about how we survive. According to the seventeenth-century English philosopher John Locke, "The state of nature has a law of na- ture to govern it which obliges every one; and reason, which is that law, teaches all mankind who will consult it,"[11] a formula- tion that clearly presupposes that people have a choice about whether to consult reason (i.e., to think). If we choose not to think, we thereby choose also to reject the requirements of human life. To the extent that we fail to engage in rational thought, we fail in the basic commitment we make when we choose to live—to live as fully as is possible for us and in such a way as to give ourselves the best chance of continuing and robust survival. Here is the root of our freedom of choice or free will, or self-directed conduct: the unavoidable and novel human capacity to activate our conceptual thinking.[12]

For a rational being to choose life—albeit in an unself-conscious, subliminal, tacit way—is tantamount to embarking upon a *rational* life, moreover one that isn't rational just now and then. This is a choice one can renege on, but to that extent one will be less than a morally good human being. To be moral means to promote one's life by acting in accordance with one's nature. To fail to do so is thus to fail to choose to be good, which is immoral.

The requirements for being morally good, then, include, first and foremost, the exercise of one's rational faculty, something that human beings must do by choice. To put it differently, moral goodness requires being as awake to the world via one's distinctive form of awareness as one can possibly be and to be guided by the fruits of this wakefulness.

It now seems clear that goodness means being in accord with one's nature. Thus, given our human nature—that of being a rational animal—it is possible to understand what it means to be a good human being.[13] It is to be in full accord with the requirement of rationality and biological health. It is clear from an understanding of human nature that one's capacity for rationality, one's distinctive humanity as it were, is actualized by choice.

So the first moral responsibility of any human being is to be mentally alert, to think rationally, and to act accordingly.[14] It is a matter of personal choice that one does what one should do; otherwise, it makes no sense that one should do it. What one cannot help but do cannot be something one *should* do. Choice is of the essence of moral responsibility.

Only the individual human being can take or neglect to take the initiative that will enable her to achieve the human moral good. Others cannot do it for her. All that can be done even for children is to provide them with good examples and shield them from gross errors. In the end, what is so unique about human life is that it is laden completely with individual moral responsibility. This is what is so tragically forgotten in our time!

HUMAN NATURE AND THE JUST COMMUNITY

Coextensive with our universal moral responsibility to live life rationally are endless diverse details, specific virtues that express one aspect or another of what it means to be rational and that can vary in relevance and importance from person to person, or even between one stage of an individual's life and another. For example, it is generally rational to be honest, productive, generous, prudent, well integrated, and courageous. These are the virtues that one will find articulated more or less intact by most moralists. What the moralists differ on is what comes first and why.

Natural rights theory is based on an ethical view in terms of which the morally good human life consists of a person living rationally. Success, excellence, or happiness (in the sense of full flourishing) *as a human being* is best pursued by living in accordance with the requirements of one's nature as a rational animal.

Only a human community, the fundamental organizing principles of which incorporate the basic facts of human moral agency, can be said to accord with human nature and be conducive to human moral goodness. Such a community can thus be characterized as just.

Just communities are not those populated only by *good* human beings.[15] That could come about by way of accident: People might just incidentally gather together and all at once be at their best, regardless of the organizational characteristics—the constitution—of their community. A good human community is one that makes moral goodness more than accidentally possible; indeed, it provides the necessary social foundation for human goodness. This is where natural rights surface.

A political community is just to the extent that it accurately reflects the requirements of human nature within the context of community life—that is, to the extent that it meets the requirements of morally sovereign individuals by means of respecting and protecting individual human rights to life, liberty, and property.

NEGATIVE HUMAN RIGHTS

That these "negative" rights can be the standards of justice for the organization of a society is often disputed on the grounds that justice requires greater activism, not merely protection from destructive acts. A just state or government would, accordingly, be "proactive"—legislate appropriate conduct, promote the good behavior of its citizens, repair past social wrongs, and the like. How, then, could the administration of a system of negative rights—protecting against intrusive acts such as murder, assault, robbery, fraud, embezzlement, and kidnapping, and adjudicating charges of the commission of such deeds—count as the maintenance of justice?

If one appreciates, however, that given the moral nature of adult human beings, it is crucial that they make decisions within their legitimate sphere of authority (the sphere circumscribed by their negative rights), then one can see why a just political and legal system would have a primarily protective rather than an activist function. Given the naturalist basis of this idea of justice and given the idea of human nature that makes the best sense, a just system must secure peace and respect for negative rights rather than promote the kinds of moral ends or objectives that only individual choices may facilitate.[16]

Consider, by contrast, the late Harvard philosopher John Rawls' conception of "justice as fairness." The central difference between the Lockean perspective on rights and the Rawlsian perspective is that for Rawls human beings are cast into situations from which they cannot extricate themselves by their own free will: Even their moral character is determined by sheer luck.[17] Accordingly, it is not possible to envision human beings as autonomous, sovereign, morally responsible, and, therefore, in need of what Robert Nozick, in response to Rawls, has argued that human beings require in a social context: namely, "moral space."[18] Rather, in the Rawlsian conception of human community life, all persons are in the same boat of having been haplessly cast into a better-or-worse life condition. Justice thus requires that we remedy the unfairness entailed by this unequal allocation of fortune *via* the establishment of equality of circumstances.[19] This involves as the substance of justice the active promotion of certain states of affairs, ends, or objectives.

FLAWS OF RAWLSIAN "JUSTICE AS FAIRNESS"

However, the very influential Rawlsian conception of human nature is unjustified. It is unable to explain the enormous advances that human beings constantly make in their own lives, their creative accomplishments, or even the philosophic and scientific innovations that characterize so much of human living. The kind of passivity that Rawls ascribes to all of us does not even square with how the Rawlsians behave: as creative political partisans of the downtrodden, the poor, and the needy.

Instead of this passive conception, a constitution of a just political community should rest on a view of humans as free, creative agents. (Of course, this is moot when political justice is not possible, e.g., in the midst of an earthquake or when people are crucially incapacitated.) The range of human creativity may not be identical, but in normal circumstances each person has ample opportunity to initiate the effort to advance his or her own life, and to become more able to cope and to succeed at the innumerable tasks that may provide fulfillment to human individuals.

Of course, conduct in line with the standards of negative rights can give rise to further, more specific rights that arise from contracts, promises, and familial relations. A child has rights that parents or equivalent agents must respect, and parents, too, have rights that children must respect.[20]

THE ROLE OF BASIC NEGATIVE RIGHTS

Rights, then, are those principles that govern some of the basic relations between human beings. The source of a specific right may vary, but the most basic source of rights is human nature, implying moral requirements for community life such that every person may be forced to abide by certain principles: It is everyone's natural right to be respected for what he is—a human being capable of choosing to live, to think, to act rationally, and to interact by respecting the rationality of all others.

The rights to life, liberty, and property state these points somewhat elliptically. What they mean is this: (1) Since it is one's basic nature to be able to choose to live, one's life (as the outcome of one's identity and essential human choice) is something that no one other than the agent is permitted to terminate or take (unless the person refuses to respect the life of another and thereby incurs self-defensive action that may kill her); (2) since the choice to live implies the commitment to choose to think and act rationally, others who have explicitly or implicitly[21] joined a community are not justified in authorizing the subversion of one's liberty to make this choice (it would be the negation and irrational denial of another's humanity to subvert her ability to choose between rational thought and action or irrational thought and action);[22] and (3) since rational choice may lead one to interact with others who also may find it rational to associate with others, the association of individuals and the results of such association (e.g., acquisition, cooperation, competition, trade, and bequeathal) may not be violated.[23]

These rights to life, liberty, and property—rights not to be murdered, assaulted, robbed, or coerced—are natural rights.

They emerge because we are human beings, because we have the power of choice to live and to flourish, and because we can best do so in societies.

The main contention wielded against the strictures of natural rights is the notion that if another lives badly, neglects his life, or suffers misfortune, help may justifiably be imposed upon him, depriving him of the freedom to choose badly that is part and parcel of the freedom to choose well. This contention is to affront or even to destroy the human dignity of the person, however needy or earnest he might be. Nor would it be moral to force someone to engage in the sort of other-assisting conduct often deemed to be honorable, like charity; coerced charity is not charity but robbery. Those who urge such measures fail to observe the requirements of human nature. That failure only appears to be helpful or necessary. Once these matters are carefully considered, it becomes clear that the alleged welfare state does not really promote human welfare at all. One cannot promote the overall welfare of human beings if one imposes conditions contrary to the requirements of human nature (except, perhaps, entirely accidentally).[24]

THE PERILS OF POSITIVE RIGHTS

One of the most powerful ideas in opposition to the free society is what political philosophers call *positive rights*. It is now usually opposed to our basic or natural *negative rights* to be free from the uninvited interventions of other persons. Positive rights, in contrast, require that members of a community be provided with services at the expense of other persons. This idea is also known, in the context of practical public policy measures, as the doctrine of entitlements.

Positive rights is also a most powerful idea set against the principles of a free economy. If people have such rights, one has no justification to refuse service to others. One may be conscripted to serve the needs and wants of other people regardless of one's own choices.

Moreover, positive rights are supposed to entitle one to services and benefits to be paid for by taxation. The idea is also used to establish the case for government regulations, which includes mainly the regulation of businesses. Free trade is, thus, constrained, at least to the extent that some significant portion of one's wealth is not one's own to allocate as one sees fit. Even if one holds that taxes must pay for government, these taxes do not pay for government but support wealth redistribution by government from some members to others in the community.

Underlying the idea of positive rights is the belief that human beings by nature owe, as a matter *of enforceable obligation,* part of their lives to other persons. In plain terms this means that governments must force us to serve our fellow human beings and that generosity or charity must not be left to individual conscience.[25] This position has even been defended on the grounds that negative rights—of the very poor, for example—entail these positive ones. Others argue that all rights are in fact positive because they are meaningless without being protected; the right to the protection of one's right to freedom, for instance, is a positive right.

In fact, there are fatal problems with all these views. The first generalizes what amounts to a rare moral emergency case into a principle of law—namely, that when some innocent people are totally helpless, they should obtain resources by stealing them—but those extraordinary circumstances do not generate any legally enforceable rights for people. Yes, those who face them might resort to stealing and might very well be forgiven because of their very limited options. But this does not generate laws granting the authority to steal!

There are others who believe that we already have positive rights to the services of the state and, thus, to the earnings of taxpayers who must pay for these services. What they fail to show is that no right to being provided with protection exists *unless* there are rights to liberty, ones that members of a community then elect to have protected and to delegate the authority to have this done. To gain protection for something presupposes that one has the right to liberty to act for that purpose, including the right to voluntarily combine with others for the purpose of gaining the protection. That original right, however, is a negative one, requiring that others abstain from intervening in one's affairs. The services of government are something people must choose to obtain by their consent to be governed, and they do not have a right to them prior to having freely established that institution.

The doctrine of positive rights has served statists well in America. The country's political system, sketched in the U.S. Declaration of Independence, was founded on a famous theory of basic negative human rights. This was originally developed by John Locke. It held that every individual human being has the unalienable right to, among other things, life, liberty, and property.

The rights Locke identified—following several centuries of political and legal thinking during which various theorists had begun to identify them more or less precisely—are negative. They require that human beings *abstain or refrain from intruding on one another.* Their existence means that no one ought to enslave another, coerce others to act in various ways, or deprive others of their property, and that each of us is justified in resisting such conduct when others engage in them. Ordinary criminal law has for centuries been grounded on bits and pieces of such a theory of individual rights: Crimes such as murder, assault, kidnapping, robbery, burglary, and trespassing all involve the violation of negative rights, requiring nothing from anyone but to abstain from coercion.

Those who wanted to retain some elements of the political outlook that Locke's position displaced, namely, the view that people belonged to the country—were, in fact, subjects of the country's head, the king or government—found a way to use the concept of human rights to advocate their essentially reactionary position. (Yes, Virginia, Karl Marx was a reactionary!) They appropriated the concept of human individual rights to mean not liberties from others but services from them. It is not that one has the right to seek happiness, for example, but that one has a right to be made happy! Positive rights are, in fact, nothing more than mislabeled preferences or values that people want the government to satisfy or attain for them. They mandate involuntary servitude!

If individual rights were no more than expressions of preferences or affirmation of values, there would be no end of conflict between our rights. An assertion of a right, for example, to private property is then nothing but a preference for owning something and as such it could be in conflict with some other right, for example, another person's similar preference to take something. That is due to the fact that these assertions would be, in the last analysis, no more than expressions of private or collective preferences.

So with the theory of positive individual rights, we find ourselves with the very unhappy situation that perfectly normal claims to having certain rights are usually in conflict. Governments, therefore, cannot just protect our rights but must pit some rights against others. Instead of government having the task of "securing these rights," government must here invoke some additional standard by which to tell which and whose rights should get protection. Since no such standards are available, the situation turns into a government not by law but by people, after all, who will decide which rights need protection and which do not.

In the Lockean natural rights classical liberal tradition, a conflict of justified and true rights claims cannot exist. In that school, when a claim is made as to someone's having a basic right, this claim may be checked out by reference to a correct understanding of human nature. The natural rights position sees human nature as resting on our correct grasp of a portion of reality. With human nature, we discover that morality and politics have emerged as new concerns in reality. In this area, we need to answer a question concerning ourselves, namely, "How ought we live?"—since we haven't the instinctual knowledge of other living beings that will just take care of living for us, nothing will avoid mistakes automatically. Furthermore, we need to answer the question, "How should we organize ourselves into communities?"

That an understanding of human nature is possible is a controversial issue. Yet skepticism here, as in many other cases, stems from a wholly unrealistic conception of what it takes to know something. Both negative and positive rights positions could fall prey to it. But if when we know something we have the clearest, most self-consistent, and most complete conceptualization possible to date (but not eternally) of what we supposedly know, we do not have warrant for general skepticism.

From the rights to life and liberty there emerges, with suitable analysis, the right to private property. It rests on two considerations: (1) Human beings require a sphere of individual or personal jurisdiction so that they may carry out their moral responsibility to choose to do the right thing; and (2) to choose to acquire valued items from the wilds or via trade is a moral responsibility, the exercise of the virtue of prudence. Acquisition, then, is something everyone ought to engage in to some degree—even a complete ascetic needs to acquire food.

Any bona fide political system must be organized in large measure so as to protect the rights to life, liberty, and, in the practical respect of both of these, private property. Thus any political rights—to be free to engage in decision making vis-à-vis political matters—must not violate those basic rights. Political rights include the right to vote, serve in government, and take part in the organization of political campaigns. Practically speaking, the exercise of one's political rights may have an impact on who governs, on various internal rules of government, and on the organization of political processes. There is, however, no political right to override anyone's right to life, liberty, or property. Any evidence of some community's legal system overriding these rights is ipso facto evidence of the corruption of that system from a bona fide political one into one of arbitrary (even if majority) rule. Indeed, one of the failings of contemporary conservative legal theory is that it does not appreciate the intimate connection between Lockean individualism and democracy. Because of this, many think that democracy may trump our basic rights.

The main reason why the founders established a government that secures our rights is that they agreed with Locke and a few others throughout human history who held that justice requires that communities fit human beings as moral agents with personal responsibility to govern their own lives. It is to protect their moral agency that warrants the establishment of governments via the consent of the governed.

With the introduction of the conceptual perversion known as positive rights, it has become impossible for government to govern by a set of consistent standards that had been provided by the theory of individual rights. Positive rights, as already noted, must be in inherent conflict—when someone is conscripted to serve another, he or she no longer can serve some of his or her own purposes or, indeed, even the purposes of many others, given the scarcity of time and skills to which others are supposedly naturally entitled. Most certainly, positive rights conflict with our basic negative rights to life, liberty, and property.

In the last analysis, the doctrine of positive rights leaves government free to impose its arbitrary standards—one day it is to help AIDS research, the next to foster the arts by supporting public broadcasting, and the following day it is to solve the problem of immoderate smoking habits among the citizenry. No standards of restraint apply—indeed, as in a fascistic system, anything goes that the leaders think is important. The only difference is that the leaders, say in the United States, still abide some modicum of democracy.

As we judge communities across the globe, we must keep in mind that what is comparatively best is not always the best that is in fact possible. Thus we can affirm the greater merits of certain political communities or countries despite their evident violation of basic rights. Just as in personal assault cases, we can distinguish between major and minor ones as well as those in between; we can also tell when communities rest on principles that render those systems entirely corrupt, those that simply are confused and messy, and those that come reasonably near to meeting the standards of basic human rights. In a formal way we already apply this method of judging communities, even if not for all purposes. We should go much farther and apply it more strictly–and substantively, including when we appraise our own country's laws.

THE GIST OF NATURAL RIGHTS THEORY

Let me summarize my points. First, natural rights theory aims to address the central question of political life: What norms should guide us in our basic relationship to other human beings? A theory of natural rights aims to answer this basic question by consulting nature, specifically human nature. It adheres to certain fundamental points about reality and our knowledge of reality, and it has a certain view about what goodness consists of: the flourishing of something in accordance with its nature. With respect to ethics or how we should morally conduct our lives, the question is what human nature amounts to and how it may be fully actualized in an individual human being who possesses the capacity to realize this human nature consistently in his or her case. By choosing life-and-rationality, one conducts oneself in a morally proper manner. A community is good—it is just—if its organizing principles are derived from the moral requirements of personal and social human life. The libertarian political philosophy stresses the primary significance of human freedom or liberty as "negative freedom," that is, the foremost significance of each person's right to liberty in the context of social or interpersonal conduct. Respecting this right—and taking measures to resist its violation—is warranted on the basis of the natural rights theory outlined in this discussion.

NO WAY TO REASONABLY DISPENSE WITH NEGATIVE HUMAN RIGHTS

Some have wanted to dispense with the idea of rights altogether, especially in the wake of so much corrupt discussion of rights, or rights talk, in our political and legal arena. Professor Heather Gert, among others, has argued for this on the grounds that each case of rights violation can, supposedly, be reduced to a matter of injuring or harming someone. So rights talk is superfluous.[26]

Yet dispensing with rights is not as easy as one might think. Violating rights is not the same as injuring or harming someone in a narrower sense. I may violate someone's rights by depriving her of the chance to make a bad choice, thus not hurting but in some sense helping her. I would (paternalistically, perhaps) impose on her something that she ought to be free to decide whether to accept or not, but doing this may not injure or harm her in any immediate manner at all. To take a choice away from a person does not always result in harming her, yet it is the major ingredient of violating her rights. *What it hampers and violates is the very capacity that is at the root of what makes a good human life possible.* Thus, if as an act of good Samaritanism, I prevent a person from injecting heroin, I may have benefited her (perhaps only temporarily), but I have, nevertheless, violated her rights.[27]

Furthermore, rights are not the kind of moral concept that arises primarily in the context of personal ethics or morality or even of small-scale social morality. Rights are general organizing norms—*meta-norms,* as Rasmussen and Den Uyl characterize them[28]—for a just community. They belong in a constitution. They serve to establish "borders" around persons to secure for them a sphere of personal jurisdiction or authority, of sovereignty. From within those borders they are able to make good judgments about how to live, including whom to invite in and whom to join on the outside. There are many other criticisms of rights theory, but I will leave these aside for now.[29]

What damaged the idea of natural rights is that no full backing for it had been articulated to start with. It rested on good insight but lacked thorough support. Even in our time, however, the most commonly voiced defense of our right to freedom merely asserts that we have such a right and argues that it is going to make us prosperous.[30] Human beings need more than this to sustain confidence in their community in the face of both domestic and international adversities.

The distinctive American polity is one that respects the moral nature of human individuals. Unlike so many other communities in human history, it has not officially sanctioned the deployment of force, threat, and intimidation to submerge the role that an adult human being must play in his or her life.[31] But this admittedly inconsistently practiced virtue of our republic is being undermined by reactionary forces. Although this reaction is understandable—people often fear personal responsibility, and others are easily tempted to exploit this fear—it must be resisted by all those who want justice and prosperity for human beings here on earth.

1

OPPOSING SENSES OF FREEDOM

It is a confusion that has hindered political debate for nearly two centuries: the notion, perpetuated in, among other places, Robert Kuttner's prominently published book *Everything for Sale: The Virtues and Limits of Markets,* that in the United States "the expansion of state constraints on the market and the expansion of the province of personal liberties have gone hand in hand."[1]

As one would expect, contemporary defenders of the classical liberal conception of the free society—that is, libertarians— scoff at this claim. No wonder. It is true that in the sphere of civil liberties there has been some improvement now and then, even by means of government, as when certain restrictions on human liberty have been legally abolished.[2] For the libertarian, however, any such improvement could not be *credited* to loss of liberty in other spheres of life! More to the point: The libertarian conception of personal liberty means exactly the opposite of the expansion of state constraints on the market. To the extent a market is thus constrained or curtailed, it is not a *free* market at all but an arena of governmental regimentation.

So Kuttner's general point seems dead wrong. Why would someone who is not mad—and having a book published by Alfred A. Knopf suggests that one is not mad, at least not obviously so—state such an out-and-out contradiction? Before one concludes that it is a contradiction, we should consider whether something else might not be afoot here.

Since the time of Georg Wilhelm Friedrich Hegel's political-philosophical writings in the early nineteenth century, and even before then (but less systematically), there has been an ambiguity in the way people use the concepts of freedom and liberty.

Consider the famous biblical saying, "The truth shall make you free," or how some folks say, "I'd really like to be free of my headache (or frustration or bad luck)." In these statements, the term "freedom" refers to the condition of being without an obstacle or impediment, regardless of the source of that impediment. It is then arguable that folks who are beset by such impediments are not free and do not enjoy liberty.

It is this sense of "freedom" that is used by Hegel and, before him, by some others—even those who wrote the Bible—in certain contexts.[3] Marx sought to elevate the notion of freedom as freedom-from-obstacles to a central political concept. He denigrated the classical liberal conception of personal liberty—freedom from obstacles imposed by other persons, freedom to act without coercive hindrance. As he says in his posthumously published *Grundrisse:*

> This kind of liberty [free competition] is thus at the same time the most complete suppression of all individual liberty and total subjugation of individuality to social conditions which take the form of material forces—and even of all-powerful objects that are independent of the individuals relating to them. The only rational answer to the deification of free competition by the middle-class prophets, or its diapolisation by the socialists, lies in its own development.[4]

Marx is saying that the kind of freedom involved in free competition—exchange unhindered by governments and criminals—is, in fact, a limiting condition on individuals.

As a determinist, Marx did not believe that individual human beings can choose to interfere with or intrude upon one another. People have no free will to initiate force against each other; only socioeconomic conditions as such pose obstacles to individual development. It is the condition of unmanaged, unplanned economic life that presents "the most complete suppression of all individual liberty and total subjugation of individuality." Why? Because some folks may not get as far as they really should get in life, economically and otherwise, while the conditions of free exchange prevail.

No doubt, in a free market many people may not achieve as much as many others, because, in a free market, the conditions enabling folks to achieve their goals depend in large part upon the choices of others. If they choose to purchase goods and services from certain producers, they thereby enhance those producers' chances of getting ahead—economically, at least. Even if the prospects for advancement in an unhampered market are indeed better than in any other, the kind of freedom thus institutionalized is not guaranteed to result in uniform advancement.

Unlike Kuttner and the Marxists, champions of the free market are not utopians. They do not fancy that the world can somehow be reengineered to achieve the dream of uniform and perfect happiness for all. The kind of obstacle-free personal liberty dreamed of by Kuttner and his ilk simply cannot be realized: People will never be free of all impediments to their various (albeit quite possibly even admirable) goals and desires. Life cannot be sustained without effort. It takes work. And luck. People must overcome hurdles at every stage, and the higher and more complex the value being pursued, the more hurdles there will be and the harder it will be to overcome them. What politics can only do is help clear the road to achievement by outlawing the arbitrary interference of our fellows and letting us get on with things.

But the dream of socialists everywhere is for some powerful agent to create a world of effortless freedom from necessity, hardship, hunger, ignorance, poverty, disease, ugliness, the indifference of others, and the like. Since that world will never arrive as long as people interact with one another voluntarily, the socialists want governments to draft us into somehow producing such a state of affairs. They really do believe that satisfaction of all of our desires can be planned top-down by the iron hand of the (sometimes democratic) state. Whereas some hope that this paradise can be achieved by democratic means (in some of his works, even Marx seemed to), men like Lenin and Stalin sought to deploy the coercive powers of government to this end directly, bypassing the formal assent of the populace. What they produced was not paradise, however. Kuttner's faith in governmental intervention, albeit not as totalitarian in temperament, is akin to such Leninist and Stalinist illusions. Keynes was similarly aligned but, according to him, for only brief periods in a country's economic development. He thought that governments could step in sometimes to advance personal goals by means of public works. This is what is referred to as demand-side government intervention.

The respective allegiances to the two opposite senses of freedom hinge upon very different basic conceptions about human nature and the sources of human wealth. Marxists, including fellow travelers like Kuttner, seem to think that their dream can be achieved by means of concentrated force because history is on a kind of inevitable march—by means of ineluctable laws—toward the utopia they envision.[5]

So the thinking goes that if only they can help history along a bit here and there—maybe not so harshly as Lenin and Stalin attempted but still with some pretty serious government tinkering—then the sort of inequalities and lack of uniform fulfillment of goals that are par for the course in the real world of free markets will be overcome and everyone will enjoy true personal liberty—freedom from want.

One lesson here is that we can't settle the argument between the Kuttnerian version of personal liberty and the classical liberal version of politics without delving deeply into the details and complexities of human life. It is not a simple issue of wherein lies the prospect of greater wealth. It is, rather, a matter of what kind of beings we are: ones facing choices that we can manage badly or well, with no guaranteed outcome, or ones on a march toward some ultimate state of uniform happiness on earth that is only temporarily derailed by such aberrant institutions as the free market and needs to be bolstered by goodly doses of government planning.

Certainly Kuttner or other mixed-economy advocates of governmentally imposed want satisfaction may not be deliberate fellow travelers of the Marxist view of history. For them, there may not be "a march toward some ultimate state of uniform happiness." What they would want is to "socially construct an ultimate state of uniform happiness" which is then derailed by the antiplanning myopia of that moral retardate, The Market. But their case rests on a view of human nature that is seriously flawed, and what exactly is wrong with it is what I am attempting to show throughout this work.

2

ETHICAL EGOISM
(OR INDIVIDUALISM)—
PERSONAL RESPONSIBILITY

One of the charges leveled against the libertarian or classical liberal conception of community life, because of the small scope it affords for government action, is that it lacks a moral base. Morality, it is often held, supports a far more interventionist government than what libertarians think just and wise.

In response to this charge, it needs to be made clear that classical egoism, an ethical position first suggested by Socrates and Aristotle and developed by Bishop Butler, Herbert Spencer, and, most recently, Ayn Rand and other Objectivists and neo-Objectivists (e.g., Eric Mack, Douglas B. Rasmussen, and myself), does provide a strong moral foundation for libertarian politics.

CLASSICAL EGOISM

Before explaining classical egoism, let's note that it is a version of individualism. The ego is the same as the individual, except in some rather esoteric discussions (e.g., those of Descartes) where the ego is some disembodied self. In a discussion of ethics, however, the more familiar term used to refer to the ego is *egoism*. Individualism tends to identify the social philosophy that rests on ethical egoism.

In any case, *classical ethical egoism* states that each person should live so as to achieve her *rational self-interest*.[1] To do so, we need a guide to conduct, principles to help us choose between alternative courses of action. The point of using "classical" to qualify ethical egoism is that this form of egoism is different from the more widely known version that dates back to Thomas Hobbes and states that every individual is entirely unique—what in philosophy is called a bare particular. Classical egoism sees every human being as a certain *kind of*—namely, human—individual.

Reiterating the gist of some points in the Introduction, as living beings, we share with other animals the value of life. But human living, unlike that of other animals, cannot be pursued automatically. We must learn to do it, and the particular life we can pursue and about which we can exercise choices is our own. By understanding *who and what we are,* we can identify the standards by which our own life can most likely be advanced properly and become a happy and successful one.

Since one's individual life is the only one a person can advance in a morally relevant way (i.e., by choice), each person should seek to do so within that person's own context and particular circumstances). In other words, each person should pursue his own individual happiness. The moral principles and virtues suited for leading a human life make this possible. The benefit that one ought to seek and obtain is, then, not subjective but objective: one's own successful, flourishing human life.

EGOISM AND OUR SOCIAL NATURE

Communitarians often claim that ethical egoism necessarily neglects our *social* nature; some social conservatives echo the charge. The claim is misguided. If, to benefit oneself as a human being, one must attend to one's own nature, and if that nature is indeed substantially social, then the pursuit of one's interest will entail the development and satisfaction of that social aspect.[2]

The primary virtue in egoistic ethics is rationality, the uniquely human (conceptual) way of being aware of and navigating the world. For any human being, success in life must be achieved in a way suited to human life. Accordingly, being *morally virtuous* consists of choosing to be as fully human as possible in one's circumstances and *to excel at being the human being one is*. Each person is a human being because of the distinctive capacity to choose to think, that is, to attend to the world rationally by way of careful and sustained principled thought; to succeed as a person, every individual needs to make that choice. Moreover, all the particular virtues that one practices must be rationally established (or at least capable of such establishment).

Classical egoism, unlike other ethical positions, considers the proper attitude in life to be informed, humanistic selfishness—not, however, pathological self-centeredness (here referred to as egotism). Pride, ambition, integrity, honesty, and other moral traits that are by nature of value to any human life are considered virtues. It is with regard to the sort of self that is proper to a human being that one ought to be selfish, not just with any sort of self; indeed, whether selfishness is good or bad depends on what the *self* is. The most reprehensible way of conducting oneself is to chronically fail to think and exercise rational judgment—to evade reality and just let oneself drift, ruled by blind impulse, thoughtless clichés, and the like. Since knowledge is indispensable for the successful realization of goals, including the central goal of happiness, a failure to exert the effort to obtain it—thus fostering error, misunderstanding, and confusion—is most disastrous to oneself and, hence, immoral. (The *social* effects of selfless failure to think are destructive, too, of course.)

Finally, in classical egoism the goal of one's happiness should be sharply distinguished from pleasure, fun, or thrills. Classical egoism sets as our primary goal to be happy, which is sustained by what we may call, somewhat laboriously, a positive reflective disposition or joyful self-awareness that results from doing well in one's life qua the individual human being one is.[3] (Of course, although the rational pursuit of well-being encompasses much more than physical pleasure, fun, or even thrills, a eudaimonistic approach to life need not exclude these when appropriate but merely seek to keep them in context.)

Although egoism is rarely advocated as such, many people act as if they accept it as their ethical system. People often strive to be happy and to succeed in career, school, marriage, and the numerous projects they undertake. Inventors are usually devoted to success, as are financiers, politicians, artists, doctors, and most productive people. Being rational is often acknowledged as a significant virtue, as when people express dismay about their own unreasonableness or thoughtlessness ("I'm sorry, I just didn't think!") or about thoughtlessness in general. But many people would doubtless be more confident and consistent in the planning and running of their lives if a rational egoism were their conscious moral doctrine rather than an unexamined default mode.

The detailed application of any bona fide moral outlook cannot be philosophically prescribed from afar—just as detailed medical advice cannot be supplied in a medical treatise without knowledge of the patient and her circumstances. Only very general principles can be identified, which must then be interpreted and implemented by individuals who, thus, either gain or lose moral credit by how they act.

Criticisms

The critics have much to say about the egoist's position. For one thing, they condemn it for its allegedly naïve view of human nature—the idea that we are born without destructive impulses and that we should simply go about achieving our natural goals. Prompted by complex and often destructive motives lying deep within us, such critics believe, egoism in practice can only lead to an unhealthy self-centeredness, hedonism, egotism, and ruthless pursuit of wealth and power.

On a more formal level, classical egoism is thought to contradict the moral criterion of universalizability. Suppose that an egoist is asked by an acquaintance what the acquaintance should do about a job opening that is in fact in his interest to pursue, but the egoist also wants the job, perhaps even desperately so. Can a consistent egoist give the correct advice? If she does so, will she not have undermined her own self-interest? The example seems to show that egoism cannot be prescribed to everyone, universally, without undermining that which it aims to support. So, for lack of a coordinating principle, egoism appears to send people on a warpath against each other. The criticism charges egoism with generating contradictory plans of action: People both should and should not do certain things. Thus, it has to fail because it leads to the view that what one should do *cannot* be done!

A further objection pertains to all the talk about happiness. Just what is this "happiness," anyway? By saying that it is the awareness and emotional experience of ourselves as being successful at living as rational people, the egoist position is said to prejudge that rational living will lead to something we ought to achieve. Is it not possible that something else besides this "happiness"—which seems very self-indulgent anyway—is worth pursuing as an ultimate goal? Could there not be far more important goals (e.g., political liberty, social justice, or being a productive member of society) that eclipse happiness? Furthermore, many rational people, scholarly and artistic achievers such as scientists, lawyers, and writers, have been notably unhappy. On the other hand, some of the most irrational and whimsical people retire in luxury to Miami Beach to live out their lives in bliss.

Rebuttals

In response to the charge of naïveté about human nature, the egoist will claim that egoism is concerned only with the essentials. The alleged naïveté in reality consists in focusing on the morally relevant aspects of every person: the capacity to freely choose to think. The misery, neurosis, cruelty, and self-destruction that often characterize human life are often explainable in terms of people's refusal to think through the requirements of their lives and their willingness to meddle in the lives of others (always for the supposed good of those others, of course). Were people to stick to doing good for themselves, honestly and rationally, much of this disarray would disappear. Nor do such factors demonstrate an inherent conflict in human nature. As long as there are well-integrated people who live with peace of mind and are happy, this possibility is established for all human life.

Suppose, furthermore, that there is an aspect of human nature, or a particular person's nature, that is both inherent and happiness-hampering—say, an inconvenient quickness to anger or even rage that is disproportionate to what provoked it, and that the person himself recognizes as undesirable. Suppose that not all of this response can be attributed to the person's past bad habits or lousy upbringing but at least in part to inherited disposition. A rational egoism would not counsel one to flourish by indulging an element in one's makeup more appropriate to the jungle than to the productive, civilized life of a human being! The goal is not to actualize each and every strand of one's nature seriatim for the sheer sake of such actualization—apart from any wider, long-range context—but to promote the ultimate goal of one's life and happiness in accordance with one's nature overall. So the advice would be to control or counter the flashes of anger in some way and prevent them if possible: to exercise one's capacity for rationality and moral choice to discover and enact a feasible solution.

If the goal is to achieve a flourishing, happy life, one must discern and seek to resolve any such problems in light of that goal, whatever their genesis. To pursue a rational way of life, a particular person need only possess the common human capacity to think; she need not be a perfect unencumbered Angel of Reason. If reason is impaired, one does not abandon reason—nor one's interest. Similarly, if a person is born with a clubfoot, we would not enjoin her to abandon the goal of getting from here to there, but to walk as well as she could.

We can answer the claim that advocating or publicly affirming ethical egoism is often self-contradictory by distinguishing between one's conduct as a moral theorist versus one's conduct when participating in a contest or economic competition. The former role commits one to advancing the general truths of ethics; the latter does not. If one, however, rationally elects to be a moral theorist, then it will be to one's benefit to advance those truths. There are contexts in which a person who is not a moral philosopher will advance such truths, too: for example, when teaching his children or explaining his philosophy of life to a prospective spouse. There are also contexts in which the moral theorist may decline to apply his moral knowledge to a particular case when doing so would benefit another at his own expense. In the example we gave above, the philosopher is not obliged to urge her economic competitor to apply for or accept the job, or even to offer any specific advice whatever. What would be wrong for the philosopher to do is to suddenly change her moral philosophy from egoism to altruism and demand that the job seeker sacrifice his actual interest for *her* own sake. So no conflict need obtain between reporting one's findings as a moral theorist and pursuing one's own rational self-interest.

If rationality is the first principle or virtue of egoism, the appropriate response when an apparent conflict of desires or moral values arises is to ask: What should I do in the face of such a conflict? What rational course of action is open to me that will then serve my long-run best interest? We should not preclude that conflicts are resolvable. Of course, if the rational answer is to cheat or lie, then so be it—that is what then would be the right choice. Sometimes cheating or lying does seem unambiguously right, as when we cheat against a crooked poker player to teach him a lesson or lie to a Nazi SS officer about the whereabouts of the Jew he is seeking. But it is very doubtful that lying would be rational in cases like the one involving rival job seekers. The rational course could be to explain that the best candidate deserves the position, so let an honest attempt to gain it be made by both and then let the chips fall where they will.[4]

As for the third point, the difficulty of *defining* happiness is not a problem of ethics but of epistemology. This difficulty confronts any complex system of ideas. It is enough to note, according to the egoist, that being happy does seem to be different from being satisfied, pleased, contented, thrilled, or fun-filled—it is the realization (and its corresponding feeling) of having carried on well in life and of having lived as a human being lives best. To be successful in the broadest sense means to do well at what people are uniquely capable of doing: guiding their lives rationally. No more skepticism is warranted here than anywhere else we deal with difficult issues.

Egoists grant that rational conduct will not *guarantee* a long and happy life; accidents can happen. The position is rather that a rational life makes reaching success more likely than does any alternative. It is wrong, moreover, to compare one person's rational life with another's irrational life without considering the full context of each life and what an alternative course of action would have wrought. True enough, some who have lived irrationally may be comparatively well off in contrast to some who live rationally—but under extremely different circumstances. There is no reason to believe that the irrational person would not have served herself better by approaching life in a more rational way, focusing on what values are appropriate for her to achieve and how best to achieve them. What is crucial to ethical egoism is that by living rationally, each person will very likely be happier and certainly savor a better self-concept than by living irrationally.

This is as far as we can go here. The only thing I wish to add is that when we speak of classical egoism, we speak not of conventional selfishness but serious, prudent, wise living with the purpose of a successful human life. One ought to conduct oneself so as to ultimately benefit oneself as the human being one is! Moreover, it must be done as a matter of free choice, which is why the free society is the best supporter of the moral life of every individual who lives in it.

3

WHY CAPITALISM
SQUARES WITH MORALITY

Why should anyone care about whether a system or its politics and economics can be reconciled with standards of human decency . . . the requirements of propriety . . . what it means to be a good person?

One answer is that people want to live moral lives, and they are most at home in a society that reflects and expresses the values that animate them as individuals.

We, as a rule, don't want to live in and support a society that clashes with our basic moral principles. We don't want to carry the burden of shame, of having to be on the defensive about the community in which we live and to which we may well be quite loyal, even if we aren't completely satisfied with it.

It would upset most of us if we had to champion, and maybe even go to war and defend, a society whose basic institutions we deem morally repugnant and objectionable. At the most basic level, the issue is one of self-esteem, but it is also a matter of pride in citizenship. We don't want to be both traitors and patriots.

That's why so many people in the academic world who favor some brand of socialism—maybe not outright Marxist-Leninist command economies, but at any rate democratic socialism, market socialism, communitarianism, or some such variation—find it impossible to be pro-American and so easy to echo the politically correct view of America as a racist, sexist, bigoted, mean, materialistic society possessed of hardly any redeeming values.

The issue is also important because a society lacking articulate moral support is so vulnerable to critical influences. It is easy to attack, to demoralize, to undermine. It can be assaulted at its roots. Moreover, it is being thus assaulted most insistently and effectively by those members of our society, as well as too many others, who, though they have the means to know better, regard capitalist institutions with the greatest disdain, if not outright hate.

The paradox is that although the intellectuals are supposed to exercise open, active minds—it's part of the job description—many will not even entertain the possibility of a more positive moral take on capitalism. When one professor learned that I would be giving a talk on the morality of capitalism (which became the basis for this chapter) he refused even to attend, adamant that capitalism could not but be bereft of moral standing. Like the pacifist who militantly steers clear of any mingling with the military, my colleague considers boycott of an opposing intellectual viewpoint to be morally superior to honest engagement with it. Of course, he probably engages with capitalist institutions everyday, anyway—like whenever he buys a new tube of toothpaste. So the boycott is probably not all-embracing. It extends only to hearing anything positive about the system that keeps him alive, only to any potentially discomfiting challenge of his anticapitalist stance.

Is capitalism immoral? It is, of course, people and not institutions who are moral or immoral per se. So to hold that institutions or systems of government or law are immoral means that we regard the activities characterizing such institutions as immoral. In the case of socialism, that means collective ownership, economic planning, and the like; in the case of capitalism, that means privately owned and run business, entrepreneurship, buying and selling, and prosperity.

Many political thinkers reject capitalism precisely because it affirms the importance of individuals and, especially, entrepreneurs. Individualism regards human beings as responsible for their own thoughts and actions and as capable of coming up with new ideas and economic plans; capitalism, they charge, unleashes this horrible ethic.

So in every department of the humanities—whether literary criticism, political philosophy, socioeconomics, or political science—the most frequent target of scholarly criticism is capitalism. The authors of the most prestigiously published books iterate over and over that capitalism and one of its most fundamental tenets, individualism, are not only wrong but, to borrow Marx's phrase, an "insipid illusion." They maintain that it is a gross error to believe that there actually exist human individuals who can do things for themselves and who deserve primary recognition in a political-legal order. They maintain that individualism is, at most, an ideological rationalization that perhaps was fleetingly useful during a period of history when folks needed to be cajoled into being productive. Now that productivity is no longer so important—as John Kenneth Galbraith declared in his famous book, *The Affluent Society*—individualism may be dismissed without further argument as an outmoded relic of the eighteenth century.

Such anticapitalism misconstrues human nature.[1] The fact is that normal individuals are able to fend for themselves, at least in some important areas. For the Marxists and fellow travelers, however, we are mere "species-beings," hitched to society at large the way limbs or organs are connected to the body. If a limb or organ should start to behave on its own, independently of the entire organism of which it is a part (i.e., the person), we would recognize that that part is diseased and defective. Similarly, say the socialists, every individual in society who opposes the ways of the community must be defective, either a lunatic or a traitor; at the least, guilty of breaking some kind of covenant they are supposedly party to (never mind what the individual chooses to do). Of course, just how we come to know the ways of the community and the right social system is conveniently left unclear.

By this view, people who spend too much money or spend it on the "wrong" things—in other words, indulge individual preferences at the alleged expense of social needs and goals—are aberrant and thus destructive to the social whole. If that's the way one thinks about human life and community life, one is indeed going to find capitalism a very defective and morally diseased sort of political economy. Capitalism is all about having people pursue their own peaceful individual goals.

So, is there any merit to capitalism from a moral perspective? Let's try to look at the question from the standpoint of common sense.

What is capitalism?

It is the political economy in which each individual has the right to private property, freedom of trade, and the pursuit of economic prosperity.

Capitalism is not all that distinguishes the political system under which capitalism flourishes. Political systems have many dimensions in addition to the economic one. The American political tradition is hospitable to capitalism and its protection of property rights—but it also protects rights to religious liberty, freedom of speech, and all sorts of legal provisions (e.g., due process).

An essential ingredient of a system of free and independent human beings is that all of them have a right to their own lives and to pursue their personal well-being. If people want to engage in trade and market themselves, their skills, their imagination, and their creativity, they may not be stopped by anyone from doing this.

At its best, the American system recognizes that individuals are sovereign and independent, and may not be compelled to submit to the demands of others, may not be enslaved by others.

This is the idea that makes capitalism and the classical liberal society that unleashes capitalism so revolutionary. In the past, before the advent of classical liberal institutions, it was generally believed that individuals belong to the tribe or clan or country or society—and, later on, even to all humanity. Something larger than and beyond the individual was always deemed more important than the individual. The individual was a mere subject, obliged always to submit to the will and the rule—supposedly a responsible will and a wise rule—of select leaders claiming superiority and occupying the head of the social body.

The revolutionary move toward capitalism took place when the notion of the individual as subject gave way to the recognition that every human being is properly in charge of his own life and that it is unnatural to live that life in bondage to others. Under individualism, one is beholden not to any state or to humanity at large but only to the judgment of one's own mind, a mind every bit as capable of judgment as that of anyone else. Whether the realm in question is religion, philosophy, or politics, it is the individual's judgment and jurisdiction over one's life that are morally central: not because there are no principles by which one ought to live but because the living must be (and can only be) done by the individual, as a matter of one's choices and commitments, in voluntary association with other individuals.

The liberty to act on one's own behalf and in accordance with one's own independent judgment is what politics should protect. Contra the views of many conservatives, the proper goal of politics is not to impose a specific moral direction upon us, but to preserve and protect the freedom that enables us to forge our own direction. We need a framework within which we can all peacefully pursue our goals and our aspirations—even when they are flawed.

One of the conditions of a morally respectable life is that one has the option to go wrong—implying not that it is good to go wrong, but that it is good to be *able to choose between right and wrong*. If one has no choice but to do what is deemed by others to be "right," one is not free to act at all. Nor can one claim moral credit for the actions one has been forced to take. When one fails because one is forced to fail, or succeeds because one is forced to succeed, we can hardly assign either moral blame or moral praise to the person for the unchosen outcome.

The requirements of moral responsibility have been understood to some extent through history, even during illiberal eras. Most religions recognize that the Kingdom of Heaven must be gained via one's own initiative, for example. Friends and neighbors may help one to choose and do what's right, but they may not force or manipulate one into doing it. Salvation and moral esteem must be earned.

This is the kind of moral position that supports capitalism as a legitimate expression of political economy. It recognizes that people need to make voluntary moral choices in order to act practically on their own behalf, on behalf of those they love or befriend, and on behalf of other members of their community or even humanity at large. Such moral choosing is possible in a social context only to the extent that individual rights, especially property rights, are protected.

The right to use and dispose of property is indispensable to the moral life of individuals and, thus, to a liberal society and the open, free markets that characterize it. Only if one has a right to private property are one's time, energy, and skills one's own to arrange—to trade, bequeath, waste, save, and so forth.

This is how capitalism gains its moral foundation. Under a regime of property rights, if one has acquired something honestly, it is possible in pursuit of a better value to openly trade it for something else. (The other party of the trade should have the same goal of pursuing his own goals by so trading, of course.) That's how trade takes place: You can't trade unless you own what you trade and are free to establish mutually acceptable terms of trade. And that's what a capitalist economy affirms, even encourages: a hurricane of trade, all protected by the right to possess and then to dispose of what one possesses as one sees fit. Nobody prohibits it; nobody *may* prohibit it.

Of course, it is possible for those who have the right to property—the right to acquire, hold, and trade valued items—to commit abuses, to be rude or unfair or even fraudulent. But any human institution will sometimes go wrong: The point is that human beings do better under one system than they do under another, that people, trade, and production fare better under capitalism than under socialism.

But economic well-being is not all that capitalism makes possible. It also promotes development in the arts, religion, and philosophy, insofar as it protects the individual's primary authority over what he or she will do. (To be sure, religion is compatible with authoritarian society; it's religious competition—the development of new religious institutions as well as fresh thought about traditional institutions and ideas—that benefits from the context of a more liberal society.) Again, I must emphasize that the fact that people are free—free in their market activities, free in their religious beliefs, free in their publishing activities, free in their political beliefs—doesn't mean they will always make the right choices. But they will be free to make the right choices—they will be free to discover what's right—and to learn from their mistakes. They will be free to take and exercise responsibility for their own lives. They will be free to be moral—or to fail at that task.

One reason why many people dislike capitalism is that they associate it with the kind of arid economic defense that denies morality altogether, claiming it to be purely subjective, a matter of personal opinion only that need be considered no further. That's wrongheaded. We need morality to live our lives successfully, and it is certainly possible to make reasonable claims about what moral choices will promote human life and what will hinder or destroy it.

Most people realize this at some level, and so they tend to be turned off by arguments for capitalism couched solely in terms of the practical economic benefits for society at large. This kind of consequentialist defense of liberty ultimately misfires. First, it does not address the issue of whether seeking wealth, in and of itself, is morally okay, honorable, and decent. Second, it does not address the fact that even free people can and often do neglect to do what is productive or virtuous. There's no guarantee, for instance, that laziness would vanish in a free society—though it sure would be harder to be a parasite indefinitely without the ability to legally rip off Peter to underwrite Paul.

But there's more to life than production in any case. It may well be true that, in the long run, leaving people free yields a more productive economy. But does this mean that a person lacks rights and is wholly unworthy to be free if she is unable or willing to be productive? Economic productivity is not an end in itself. It serves the more fundamental and greater end of human life.

Thus, defenders of capitalism on consequentialist grounds cannot show why it is wrong, in individual cases, to intrude on people when they do something against the will of those who would intrude. Knowing about the economic consequences of illiberal rule is important—it's important to know that it's harder to make a living (or "grow the economy") when the state crushes production—but this is only part of the story, and not too inspiring absent a wider moral context.

So what about that moral defense? What points would a moral defense of capitalism have to touch on?

One of the charges continuously leveled at capitalism's defenders is that they are simply ideologues who have concocted a facile rationalization for their insidious pursuit of profit. This characterization substitutes character assassination for argument. For my own part, I certainly didn't come to this country with a built-in disposition to seek profit, but I did want to learn the difference between a communist country like Hungary and a relatively free one like America. I wanted to know why one system is patently more hospitable to human life than the other.

During a recent lecture tour in Prague, Budapest, and other cities in former Soviet bloc countries, I asked students there: Is it still the case in Eastern Europe and elsewhere that people see America as a place where individuals can set their own course and where they have really a chance to do things for themselves? All of these students, without fail, testified that that's still the vision of America that most people carry around in their hearts and minds.

Are they all wrong? Are the bulk of Western intellectuals right? Are the literary critics, political scientists, and philosophers right who believe that America's largely capitalist system is crass, heartless, devious, and exploitative? Did I—as well as millions of others—make this awesome choice because I'm seeking a decadent, corrupt life? Did I want to escape a good regime in favor of a licentious, libertine system that so many intellectuals claim is so destructive of an honorable human life? Or did I have the right idea that more-or-less capitalist societies are more just than the socialist or authoritarian ones, more suited to human flourishing?

To find out, I realized that I had to first ask the question: What does it mean to *be* a human being? What is human nature? I also considered that what distinguishes human beings from all other living creatures is our capacity to make a free choice and the responsibility, which cannot be bartered or disowned, to do it right. Any theory of what constitutes a just social system must take these facts of our nature into account.

As I've noted before, all other animals live largely instinctively. There might be a few chimps or porpoises who can be dragged into a lab and trained to imitate human behavior, but it is human beings who are the prime movers even here; such relatively sophisticated animals manage to simulate a few rudimentary elements of human behavior only after months of being badgered into it. For the most part, animals behave in accordance with built-in, instinctual mechanisms.

By contrast, humans possess a conceptual consciousness, the level of consciousness that doesn't function automatically. As anyone knows who has had anything to do with teaching, students don't think automatically. They have to make the choice to think; they have to make the choice to put their minds into gear. That is the primary, rock-bottom choice that all human beings must make in order to be creative at all in using our peculiar form of consciousness, and to ascend from merely perceptual or sensual beings to thinking ones. This choice cannot be initiated "once and for all"; it must be sustained. We must commit to being alert and thoughtfully attentive of the world and ourselves at every important turn.

From the very beginning of human life, there had to be some initiative. There had to be some surge forward. Those who didn't do so consistently enough fell behind and had to be sustained by their fellows until they either recovered or perished. Life can be full of accidents, but all in all, what makes humans unique is that we can and must advance ourselves by our own initiative. We can and must ignite the motor of our own lives.

Of course, there are exceptions. There are cases of people who are born defective and who are unable to do anything about it. That's where compassion comes in, and generosity and charity and good will and giving a helping hand—but not as a permanent condition of our lives. Moreover, such attitudes and conduct toward them cannot properly be forced, either, by government or other coercive agents. If our own individual lives are important and worth sustaining, our ability to judge and to act on our judgments must be left unimpeded.

Human beings are creators and producers, and we have to look out for ourselves. If we don't, no others will—not unless we enslave them (a counterproductive alternative at best) or rely indefinitely on their charity and good will.

To be effective navigators of our lives, we need what philosopher Robert Nozick calls "moral space," a sphere of exclusive jurisdiction. We need a certain measure of sovereignty, of autonomy. That doesn't mean we are isolated atoms or hermits, just that for some of the most crucial decisions of our lives, other people must ask permission to participate. If we don't have that veto power, our moral worth cannot be developed and recognized by others as indeed *our* worth. Then we are obliged always to serve as members of committees in every decision we make, no matter how directly it may pertain to our own individual well-being and fate; every bad or good decision we make is really the decision of a group.

If the moral world were indeed like that, nobody would be responsible for his own actions in any fundamental sense; nobody could be *held* responsible. Not the rapist, not the architect, not Mozart, not Beethoven, not Charles Manson, not Adolf Hitler, not Albert Schweitzer, and not Mother Teresa. They would all be simply products of some committee: a tribe, a clan, a community, a society. This all-governing committee would itself be but a product of forces over which no one has control and for which no one in particular could be held responsible.

Private property rights are a concrete legal implementation of the concept of moral space: They allow me to attain, keep, and use the various "props" that help me to live, props acquired through my own effort and the good will of others, maybe through their gifts, maybe through trade, maybe through good fortune. Models, for example, are fortunate to have inherited their beauty genetically (though perhaps in a few cases it's all done with makeup and mirrors). But this benefit is still properly theirs to manage and negotiate, and the principle of private property rights (an incarnation of the right to life) enables them to do so.

One of the first questions of politics is, or should be: Are we going to be free to act as moral agents in a social context? Though surrounded by millions of people, are we going to enjoy a moral space within which we can function as sovereign judges and actors? For if that space is not secure, then our moral agency is not secure and we cannot operate as independent, sovereign, moral agents. Then we are mere subjects of the will of others who exert power over us, whether king, tribal chief, democratic assembly, or autocratic central committee. And that's no fun, to say the least.

If others are legally authorized to push us around, to grab or govern our private property, or to throw it open to all comers, the contours of our moral responsibility become blurred. Consider, for example, how environmental problems often arise in society, in part because many firms exploit the commons (i.e., the commonly held resources to which everyone is supposed to enjoy equal right but to which no one holds actual title). Under such circumstances, people are able enjoy the immediate benefits of usage but need not incur the immediate costs of resource depletion (as would a private owner), and thus they have no incentive to maintain the resources. Those making use of the resources are not fully accountable for how they behave there.

Indeed, it's the politicians who dole out the permission by yielding to pressure from constituents; it's the judges who rule in favor of making a certain public ground available to the people. The agents of the government set up the whole situation. So although firms may catch the blame for any resource depletion or spoilage, they cannot justly regard themselves as primarily guilty. They just don't have any way to gauge how much of that public resource they "really" have a right to and are responsible for. And they may well, and justifiably, see themselves as responsible people just the same. For they have taken advantage of whatever resources are made available to them to advance a goal that they rightly consider perfectly legitimate. This is the goal of maximizing their profits and those of their stockholders, who may include many hundreds or thousands of people who trusted them with the responsibility of giving them a return on their investments.

Although public funding is not often understood as a "tragedy of the commons," the same incentives motivate those lobbying for public funds for the arts, sciences, education, or whatnot. They too regard the public realm—in this case, the treasuries of their governments—as bottomless wells to be dipped into without limit and without personal costs (except those entailed in filling out the application form). They, too, though perhaps with less excuse, do not see themselves as exploitative.

All the applicants for grants and subsidies have projects they believe in and want to promote. If the public coffers are there for them to use, why not go ahead and do so? This then leads to everyone using the resources with abandon, regardless of which portion should really go for their tasks (if the proper allotment could even be determined under such circumstances, which it can't). The only ones who might abstain are those who reject a government handout on moral principle. And so the country accumulates trillions of dollars of debt. Thus another instance of the tragedy of the commons!

What makes all this scrambling for public help possible is a system that has socialized a great deal of resources and thus has often made it impossible to distinguish between what is my proper realm of operations and what is your proper realm of operations.

It doesn't have to be this way.

If we compare the administration of Disneyland grounds to the administration of our public beach, or the superior caution a politician exercises when dealing with her personal budget to the recklessness with which she splurges the public budget, the point is clear. On the public beach, people just throw stuff around; if life happens to call them elsewhere, they can just leave without bothering to clean up. Nor do they ever come back later to make things tidy. Yet, every evening Disneyland is cleaned up. Why? Because it's privately owned and because the owners profit from maintaining consistently clean grounds; they have a direct responsibility of a kind that visitors to the public beach do not have. There is a greater propensity, albeit no guarantee, to deal with the resources responsibly when private property is involved.

This is one function of private property rights, from a moral point of view. These rights enable a person to live his life with the awareness and on the basis that he first and foremost is responsible for that life. Property rights also make it possible for others to notice when someone intrudes or takes advantage without permission, and to do something about it if necessary. That's a crucial moral benefit of capitalism. It systematically enables people to be moral agents—a capacity that is systematically usurped in a socialized system.

In *To Build a Castle,* an account of Soviet society, Vladimir Bukovsky depicts the crumpled condition of human morality under socialism. Everybody is suspicious of everybody. Everybody is envious of everybody. Nobody can tell with certainty who did what, where, and to whom; nobody knows how to distinguish between the good and the bad. Everyone is under indictment, simultaneously responsible and not responsible. You can't be responsible, because there is no private domain, no clearly defined scope for individual responsibility. That kind of social existence is not merely dog-eat-dog. It's soul-eat-soul.

Capitalism, by contrast, clears the moral decks. Although every adult is not necessarily out for herself alone under capitalism, she alone is at least unambiguously responsible for her own conduct. That doesn't mean there is never any fuzziness of moral boundaries in a liberal society; it does mean, however, that folks have the means to steer clear of the chronic moral blurring of the illiberal society.

In addition to making moral responsibility possible to begin with, capitalism also provides scope for the cardinal virtue of prudence, which one might call the first practical virtue.

For this life, here on Earth, prudence is an indispensable virtue. In order to be a good human being and live a successful human life—so that one's life is lived honorably, honestly, decently, productively, industriously, frugally, and responsibly—one must be prudent. Prudence means practical wisdom. It is the virtue of promoting one's life well, of getting things done.

We are implicitly aware of this virtue when we criticize someone for reckless driving or wasting his life away. We're aware of it when we criticize others or ourselves for throwing things away that shouldn't be thrown away, or for being careless in our spending habits or sloppy in our retirement planning.

What enables one to act prudently, in a social context? What is the institutional manifestation of the virtue? It is the market itself: commerce and its professional manifestation, business. It is the brokers, security analysts, consultants, and executives of corporations to whom we turn when we want what I want to call wealth care—serious professional care for our economic well-being, and it is every other participant in the marketplace who helps us get done what needs doing. They all help us live a prudent life—an effective life.

You could not live your life prudently unless you have the institution of private property, at least to some degree. You could not use your own judgment to allocate resources. Rather, some group or leader would foist the choices on you, and your own rational judgment would be pointless unless the group leader condescended to give you the nod. You could not exercise the virtue of prudence in that case. You could sort of mimic it, exercise it as well as you could under chronically ambiguous circumstances—that moral bog of the collectivist society.

It is true enough that in most collectivized groups, whether a tribe or a major socialist country, there are shadow marketplaces, black markets. Markets are hard to stamp out completely. Even in the most diligently communal community, one can still distinguish one's own toothbrush or apartment or furniture or clothing from somebody else's. One can still talk about thine and mine in a de facto, surreptitious way, even when the law does not recognize private property rights. But, for the larger, complicated aspects of social life, that option isn't tenable. Skulking and firm handshakes between desperate strangers only take you so far. At a certain point in the production process, it's nice to be able to rely on the legality of what one is doing and not to have to waste precious time, ingenuity, and angst covering up what one is doing (or bribing all the in-the-know bureaucrats).

Even in a relatively free country like the United States, with its welfare state and copious taxes and regulations, a lot of what we might be able to do for ourselves and those we love is taken out of our hands. It's regimented or it's banned—by city, state, or federal entities. These entities often behave like paternalistic manipulators rather than rights protectors, but their proper job is the latter.

Sad to say, democracy has devolved into a kind of fascism under which everybody can vote on practically everything, with the majority authorized to impose its will on practically every matter that comes up for discussion. If there's a large enough constituency that wants something done—force you to stop smoking, change the configuration of your front yard, raze your house to make way for a highway—they need merely combine to vote for it, or delegate the power to the Supreme Representative to do it for them. There's insufficient protection of our private property, our individuality, and our private judgment these days. That means that our very moral nature is being violated.

But this kind of indictment isn't the report card we usually get. Instead, we're told how horribly exploitative capitalism is, how hedonistic it is or how it rapes the planet. Even supporters are too eager to set aside the moral aspects of the matter and too eager to stress, exclusively, capitalism's capacity to produce a lot of wealth, satisfy extant preferences, and so forth.

Out of this moral vacuum arises the belief that capitalists are mere morally vacuous profiteers. The next move is to castigate them as "money-grubbing scum," to borrow David Letterman's flattering characterization. (The money-grubbing writers and actors and late-night comedians, of course, are all saints.) Although Letterman may not really mean it, the crack resonates precisely because there are so many capitalists who are.

Now there is a problem, of course, with all the terrible press that capitalism receives. It's not objective. Most of those who write it are afflicted by a deep-seated anticapitalist bias. They think commerce is crass and mean, whereas the truly noble activities are the arts, sciences, and education. (Noble, at least, until they become tainted by contact with other human beings through the mechanisms of the market process, one must suppose. *The Iliad* may have been high art before it became widely available in a cheap paperback edition, but what about now?)

Why do the intellectuals harbor this seemingly inexplicable bias—inexplicable, at least, from the standpoint of common sense and the value of human survival?

Part of the reason is the very long legacy in Western culture that exalts "pure" activities of the mind—especially articulate, intellectual activities—as intrinsically more honorable and decent than commercial activities. From Plato's *Republic* to Arthur Miller's *Death of a Salesman,* commerce (despite the keen intelligence it often requires and rewards) has been denigrated. Everything from high drama to routine cop shows is full of corporate executives acting underhandedly and knocking off those they don't like. Typically, the conniving business executives are the worse for comparison with the heroic public-spirited public servant who, outraged by all the untrammeled greed and ambition, strives to thwart them.

This ingrained cultural legacy holds that the human mind or spirit is far more important than anything else about human beings, that the body and its ravenous pursuits are even contemptible. It's somewhat like our pre-1960s attitude toward sex, which still lingers. We can't do without it, but we're not quite proud of it.

The spirit of the Fourteenth Amendment of the U.S. Constitution, which mandates equality under the law, is certainly not respected in this context. The First Amendment gives almost absolute freedom to those of us who write and speak, but business is relentlessly hounded, regulated, and subjected to prior restraint. The press and the religious community, which enjoy this unequal treatment under the law, tend to see nothing unjust about their preferential treatment.

It's true that a society in which all were concerned *only* with commerce would be an impoverished one—in other words, if it lacked arts, sports, community, philosophy, and spiritual concerns—and if all the material goods of a society were just empty husks that never embodied or facilitated values that touched the soul. Yet a capitalist society is much more hospitable than any other society for spiritual purposes, too. Consider, for instance, that under capitalism and its cardinal principle of the right to private property, a church enjoys a sanctuary upon which no one may lawfully intrude. (Though, to be sure, even the protection awarded such preferred "spiritual" pursuits as religion and journalism is being undercut nowadays: The Reverend Sun Myung Moon has been hounded endlessly by the IRS, because he was not one of the established religions. Moreover, the Securities and Exchange Commission (SEC) did its darnedest to regulate business newsletters and almost got away with it. The material and the spiritual usually come in a package, you see; the disdain for one can thus easily be deployed as a wedge to make inroads against the other.)

I would argue that bona fide morality favors a consistent free market capitalist system of law. If there are dangers or temptations faced by members of society, let the various institutions that can develop among free peoples take on the job of resisting and counteracting those temptations. Let individuals and their various voluntary organizations, not governments, take care of our souls, our medical needs, and the preservation of monuments or historical buildings or wilderness parks and the rest. Let those things be taken care of by people in their voluntary interaction, not by some arrogant elite, whether self-chosen or democratically chosen. Let the legal authorities act like referees on the playing field, making sure the basic rules are upheld but involving themselves in no aspects of the actual game lest their integrity be compromised.

What is glorious about a system in which private property is fundamentally respected is that you are free to embark upon your way of life, provided you do not foist your mistakes and troubles on others. You can then live any kind of peaceful life you want, and your failures and successes will belong to you and those who choose to accompany you. In this way, capitalism allows us to treat our lives as precious, which they are.

And if that's not a spiritual good, what could be?

4

IMMIGRATION INTO
A FREE SOCIETY

THE PROBLEM OF IMMIGRATION

What should be a free country's policy be toward foreigners who wish to live there? This may appear to be a fairly simple question but it involves many complications. To start with, what exactly is a free country? What is a policy? What precisely are foreigners?

In this discussion I will construe a free country to be a contiguous geographical region, the rightful occupants of which have chosen, individually and mutually, to be governed by a common system of laws and their administrators. There would be full consent of the governed to the basic principles of the government and its constitution, and everyone would have the right to take part in the selection of the administrators whose authority would be fully circumscribed by the provisions of the constitution—in other words, administrators would have no special authority that the citizens cannot possess.

A policy of such a country would be legal guidelines that prescribe how to deal with certain public concerns. To join such a country would be to some extent a public concern, applying to all who are not but wish to become members of the citizenry. Such people who aren't citizens of the country are foreigners relative to the citizens of the country.

To immigrate into a country would amount to abiding by the policy that should guide the process of becoming a citizen of a country, and we are here interested in immigration into a free society. How would that be done?

Proper Immigration

The right immigration policy for a free country, to put it bluntly at first, should be this: *Those who can demonstrate that they aren't under indictment for any kind of violent crime, have the economic means—a job, property, or both in the free country they choose to join—and take an oath to respect the rights of everyone should be accepted as citizens.*

In a free country this would mean that they are self-supporting, not dependent upon obtaining funds from others for their survival. Now, this is not what one might call a recklessly "open door" policy on immigration but one that is open in a prudent, responsible fashion. Not just anyone could become a citizen, true enough. There is, however, no basic right to be accepted as a neighbor in any society—one needs to earn admission.

What reasons can be given for accepting the above? The argument goes like this: To acquire property, one needs either to find and develop valued items or to voluntarily obtain them from others who have done the same. This applies to acquiring a residence and livelihood. If those acquisitions were made properly, without coercion or fraud, one would become a fellow citizen, a neighbor.

Modeling Immigration

Consider, as a possible model for immigration, joining a so-called gated community. People often seek entry there either to visit folks who live there or to explore the possibility of and eventually purchasing or leasing a home. In such cases they may enter only if given permission by those who own the place—an occupied home or one that is for lease or sale. They would have to leave if the owners withdrew permission. Once, however, they meet their terms and become lessees or owners, they can live in the community.

A free society may well be modeled on such a gated community. Immigration would be predicated on the permission to either visit someone (an employer or friend) or to purchase a residence. The general precondition, then, of immigration into a free society is self-sufficiency and voluntary relationship with those who are already there.

DOWN TO SOME CURRENT CONCERNS

Of course, many questions have arisen in connection with immigration policies in the United States and elsewhere, and it will be useful to address at least some of them based on the general position sketched above.

Is Cultural Identity Necessary?

To start with, does an ongoing viable political community require a sense of "identity" based on more or less common cultural attributes? Is this kind of "anti-immigration" argument essentially collectivist? Such an issue has been raised by, among others, Patrick Buchanan, one of the Republican presidential aspirants in 1996.

If by "identity" we have in mind some unifying set of values that bear on public policy and human interaction, in general, there is reason to believe that the anti-immigration argument tied to this concern has some merit, although the matter is fully manageable by reference to the criminal record or lack thereof of the prospective immigrant, as well as his or her willingness to swear to uphold the law in the country to which he or she aims to immigrate. Consider, for example, that one may wish to immigrate to the United States while also committed to the tenets of Islam, Roman Catholicism, or even, to use a more exotic example, serious bullfighting. If, as it should be, there are no laws prohibiting religious affiliations in a free society nor any prohibiting the use of animals for sport, then there will be no problem with someone with such commitments coming to that free country. The constitution of such a country makes ample room for those who are economically self-sufficient to continue to follow their faith or sporting habits. Should, however, a prospective immigrant believe in, say, the Ghanaian practice of sacrificing a ten-year-old virgin to a local priest who believes that her father sinned and that the young girl needs to pay for those sins, or should someone aspire to join a free society with the objective of coercing others to avoid eating meat because cows are sacred, they could not honestly swear to live by the laws of the country and could not, then, come and become its citizens.

We might put it this way: A minimalist identity of fundamental beliefs in individual human rights is required of prospective immigrants. The precise philosophical or religious source of such a belief, however, is not relevant, nor need such prospective immigrants become committed practitioners of the religious and cultural customs and rituals of the bulk of the existing population. A free society respects individuality and cultural variety provided that all of these take place within the framework of a system of laws that protect individual human rights to life, liberty, and property.

Immigration and Democracy

What effect, however, does today's mass democracy have on the issue of immigration? Currently, whoever is in control of the state apparatus, through elections, can dispose of the wealth of all citizens. Is this an argument for limiting immigration?

We, of course, live in what I have dubbed a democratic fascist state, one wherein the majority of voters can have their way with the law with nearly no restraint at all. The U.S. Supreme Court is no bulwark against this any longer, after decades of deconstruction of the U.S. Federal Constitution and many state constitutions. What, if anything, can be done to set immigration aright in this context?

There is reason to think that limiting immigration will not help at all; indeed, it would be hypocritical to have a welfare state, which is supposedly dedicated to assisting those in dire straits, exclude people outside of the country from benefiting from its wealth distribution. In any case, however, the welfare state is such a confusing mess of contradictions that one cannot derive from its tenets any consistent policy about anything, including immigration.

Are Europeans to Be Preferred?

Is it, furthermore, conceivable that immigration should be limited, for contingent political reasons, to Europeans plus others who have certain skills and backgrounds?

As discussed in the previous paragraphs, the only matter that should concern citizens about prospective citizens is whether they can sustain themselves without becoming burdens on others and whether they are committed to living in terms of the laws of a free society. Provisions to ascertain such matters would be appropriate but to demand any further declarations or loyalties would be a violation of the rights of those prospective immigrants. This does, of course, tend to favor Europeans in the tradition of classical liberal ideals and ideas, although that, too, is just a loose association that has innumerable exceptions. It is the substance of commitments, not the origin of those committed, that matters in this as in many other areas of social life.

I should add here that the suggestion that ethnicity should count for much is confused: It is unclear what ethnicity is in an age of widespread intermarriage among people of a great variety of ethnic origins, not to mention the intermarriage and procreation of those who already come from mixed parentage. (I, for example, have a German mother and a father who came either from Scotland or Slovakia.)

Nearly everyone in Europe, not to mention the United States, is now of mixed parentage—in relatively free societies,

the dreams of Pat Buchanan and his many enthusiastic supporters are impossible to implement. What one can do is to
apply the test of loyalty to legal principles, which is what taking an oath in support of the U.S. Constitution approximates.
The trouble is, then, with the current content of that document and how courts interpret it, not with immigration policy as such. The ethnic cleansing implicit in the Buchanan
doctrine is not only in violation of cherished and true American principles of justice—whereby individuals are supposed
to be judged on the content of their character, not by the
color of their skin or the "purity" of their blood—but totally
impracticable.

Does an Open Door Policy Favor a
Given American Political Party?

We can finally address a concern of Peter Brimelow's, raised in
his book *Alien Nation* (Random House, 1995) and in various essays, for example, in the conservative magazine *National Review.*
Of course, this concern is nothing new—in America, there has
been a strong movement for over a century against opening the
country to immigration by non-Anglo-Saxon, nonwhite people. Around the end of the nineteenth century there were the
goo-goos, intellectuals, and political activists who wanted
America to remain loyal to George Washington's idea of very
limited foreign entanglements not so much because this would
be unjustly imperialistic but because annexing such places as the
Philippines and Cuba would open the country "to the influx of
inferior races."

Brimelow's specific concern is a bit similar, namely, that an
open borders policy would make the election of Republicans
difficult if not impossible in the future. He strongly suggests that
those who would enter the country would most likely vote for
a party, such as the Democrats, that is fully committed to ex-
panding the welfare state and adheres, in essence, to democratic
socialism or at least economic democracy (the view that Ralph
Nader promotes).

Certainly there may be something to this, given the propensity of governments to wrest their power by means of wealth redistribution. First, such a policy violates the tenets of a bona fide free society. Second, once those tenets are systematically violated—in other words, their violation is embodied in the legal system—there is what might be called a "deuces wild" situation in the country. This follows from a well-known principle of formal logic: Once a contradiction enters a line of argument or reasoning or enters an action-guiding system such as a legal order, nothing can be excluded from it on principle. This means that although one group may be favored in immigration for a period, another might be for another; this means that, yes, Republicans might not meet with the approval of those who wish to enter the United States for the sake of becoming welfare recipients, if the country's policies, because of popular sentiment to which politicians yield, change toward, say, fundamentalism in religion or militarism that in turn may favor Republicans. There is, in short, some short-term validity to the fears of Republicans but this could easily change in line with the winds of opinion.

In the main, Brimelow and the goo-goos' concerns border on racism in any case, but even if they are mostly an expression of real political problems having to do with how indigent immigrants may vote, they do not apply to the truly free, libertarian polity in which no wealth redistribution could occur.

CONCLUDING THOUGHTS ON IMMIGRATION

If one holds that a certain system of laws is required to establish, protect, and maintain justice in a human community, one will also hold that once there are serious, systemic compromises in that system of laws, matters will go haywire and a gradual situation of "anything goes" will develop on any front of social life. Tyrannies beget tyrannies, small ones greater ones, and the only way to resist this is a vigilant insistence on the reestablishment or at least an approximation of the system of laws that serves justice. The libertarian idea is that a consistent system of law guided by the principles of individual human rights serves justice best, including in the area of immigration policy. Once that system is abandoned, there is not much one can do except strive to get it back, or get closer to it.

We might add here that immigration policies that stress the issues I touched upon above—striving for criteria of self-sufficiency and absence of criminal intent—should sustain an optimal approach even in the midst of the widespread confusions engendered by the welfare state that is our current reality in most Western countries, including the United States.

5

MILITARY DEFENSE OF
THE FREE SOCIETY

BASIC QUESTIONS OF MILITARY POLICY

We now reach a concern that is central to libertarian public policy: the place of force in dealing with other countries. What are the ethical foundations for such interactions? To what extent may one country interfere with the conduct of another?

The libertarian advances a public policy of what might best be dubbed *defensivism* in the realm of international military relations. It is only this part of the story that will be touched upon here, not the entire range of diplomacy. However, this is the most important portion of this topic, at least from the libertarian perspective. When is force to be used, if ever, toward another country? This is the central question of military ethics. Everything else rests on what its answer comes to.

ETHICS IN GENERAL

The most basic question, perhaps, is, What ought to be the ethics of international intervention such that it is consistent with general precepts of human morality and politics? The first point to make is that ethics is only possible if human beings possess free will. For, as is sometimes said, "ought" implies "can."[1]

It is one of the tragedies and confusions of our age that although much effort is spent on considering what we ought to and ought not to do, individually and collectively, the basic conception of human nature many of us embrace makes the issue entirely moot. We tend to prefer to explain human behavior by reference to causes or variables and to deny persons the capacity to make basic choices. Instead, everyone is addicted to and victimized by factors other than his or her free will. Such a view is incompatible with ethical considerations.

Second, when we consider ethics, we are essentially involved in answering a question that everyone asks either explicitly or implicitly, namely, How should I act? or, How should I live? or, What standards should guide my conduct? An ethical theory is a systematic answer to this question, one that we all answer somewhat ad hoc, as per our common sense, all the time.

In this respect, ethics is not that different from other disciplines in which we have initial, approximate answers to our questions. The difference is that not many of us ask such questions about physics, chemistry, biology, or even sociology. But ethics concerns us all as human beings. Ethical theory is of universal human concern. The most basic answer to its question must apply to us all in relationship to living a human life. The various ethical theories such as hedonism, utilitarianism, egoism, altruism, Kantian ethics, and Aristotelian ethics are our more focused, systematic answers to the question that gives rise to ethics.

ROLE ETHICS

We can also focus our ethical concerns on special roles that we play in our lives as parents, friends, colleagues, professionals, citizens, and athletes. Thus ethics divides into role ethics or the ethics of different human endeavors. Being a parent, a friend, or someone with a profession or role in life narrows the focus. These different endeavors spell out in more specific terms what it means for a human being to live, and thus they provide ethical theories with more content than those theories otherwise possess. Just living a human life is a very general, broad task with few specifics and much diversity based on the equally essential element of the individuality as well as the specialization of such a life.

Nevertheless, at no point would the specifics of a role that a human being may have assumed in life justify contradicting the general theory that best addresses the question that gives ethics its function in the first place. Thus the ethics of being a parent would not ever come into conflict with ethics as such—any more than the physics of light or electrons would ever be in conflict with physics as such.[2] This is a metaphysical matter that pervades all of existence, not excluding ethics: No contradictions can exist.

It may appear otherwise. Some roles that we assume in life—that of the soldier or the spy, for instance—seem to require conduct from us that conflicts with morality. A soldier must at times kill, a spy lie. Indeed, in most roles and professions we seem to overemphasize some objectives, and thus the virtues and vices relevant to it, at least temporarily. But the reason it appears that the roles contradict morality is that morality is often regarded in a loose, unsystematic fashion and the virtues subsumed under ordinary morality are not ranked in any order. A precise ordering or ranking of the virtues is not needed until we find different moral principles in conflict: loyalty to friends with honesty, charity with justice, justice with generosity, and courage with prudence. With theories, we set priorities and rank the virtues from the most to the least significant. Thus a spy might be justified in lying if the protection of the society that he or she serves requires this or if justice demands it. A soldier may need to hurt others in order to uphold justice and may stress courage but not charity. A person in business may carry on prudently and not address problems of justice or fairness because of the focus of his or her profession. The need for rigor only arises when we face serious conflicts, and the problem is not any different in other disciplines: We are able to get by with amateurish physics, chemistry, history, and law until we meet up with contradictions and dilemmas. Then the need for greater rigor arises.

The major problem with professional ethics such as business, military, medical, legal, or educational ethics is that these are rarely placed within the framework of a larger ethical system.[3] In our time, when intuitionism is so prominent, this is especially troubling. Just as with the ethics of medicine, police work, or the military profession, we are dealing with fields of human activity often focused on extreme circumstances and emergencies. That itself has bearing on the nature of the special ethics. Yet even here it is vital that the ranking achieved with the general ethical theory be kept clearly in mind. Without it, we must become confused.[4]

MILITARY PROFESSIONAL ETHICS

What are the ethical and political guidelines that govern international military intervention? Since we are ultimately inquiring about how human beings ought to act toward one another, we can begin the inquiry at the level of social ethics. We can begin with how we ought to interact with our fellow human beings, which in this instance are strangers in contrast to next of kin or friends. The most basic answer to that question is to be found in a theory of individual rights.

When human beings who are not intimates of one another interact, their central guiding principle depends on what kind of beings they are. Since human beings are moral agents, the first thing to consider about them is whether interacting with them intrudes upon them as choice-making, moral agents. Morality requires, first and foremost, a sphere of personal jurisdiction.

At this point, someone might think we are far from issues concerning international intervention, yet that would be a mistake. Indeed, the notion of peaceful national self-determination is entirely dependent, normatively, on the fact that individual human beings are moral agents in need of a sphere of personal jurisdiction that makes their self-determination possible. Nations are not moral agents. The call for peaceful national self-determination must, therefore, be understood as the call for the peaceful personal self-determination of members of a given community.

From this it follows, almost directly, that if a nation is such that its self-determination is indeed that of the combined self-determination of its citizenry, any intervention in its affairs would be no different from interfering with an individual who has embarked on self-determination without violating the personal spheres of others. Interaction with the people of such a nation may only be on peaceful terms voluntarily agreed to by all parties.

A fairly easy issue has to do with when a nation abandons self-determination and embarks upon determining the affairs of others who have not consented. Thus when one nation attempts to act aggressively toward another, interaction with it should follow the ethics of self-defense. Whatever is needed to repel the aggressor is ethically permitted and indeed is often required. People have not only the right but also the responsibility to defend themselves, unless doing so would produce worse results than the aggression itself.

MILITARY ETHICAL MUDDLES

The difficulty begins when one of two sorts of situations obtain: (1) There is an external situation in which a nation acts aggressively toward another that is unable to defend itself and calls upon yet another nation to lend support to its defense; or (2) there is an internal situation in which a nation does not actually practice self-determination but exhibits some form of tyranny, whereby some members of the nation prevent others from engaging in self-determination.

In an external situation involving international aggression, it makes no difference whether the aggressor country is itself self-determined or a tyranny, for its aggression is unjustified in either case. Thus if a country of citizens with a given religious, ethnic, or cultural tradition is completely united in its efforts to subdue another country, the culprit is simple to identify. Sometimes, however, a country may take military action against another when either both countries internally violate the principle of self-determination or the aggressor country is a truly self-determined country but the target is not. When both violate the principle of self-determination, there is no question that lending a hand to either country would be wrong unless the disparity of tyrannies is very significant. Intervention would only be right when the less evil of the two countries is significantly better. When only one of the countries is self-determined, the question centers on whether the tyranny of the other is powerful enough to resist the justified intervention (for instance, in support of liberating the tyrannized among the citizenry) and whether the aid is promised in the first place by some military agreement.

In an internal situation involving intranational oppression and injustice, we face the case we might examine at the micro level as follows: Suppose that A has legitimately contracted his or her security services to party P, and in the course of performing those services one notices that another party, C, is acting aggressively toward yet another party, D. Should A go to the aid of D? The answer is "no" unless it does not interfere with the performance of the original contract between A and P and does not establish a precedent or a long-term commitment that would distract from the original commitment.

We have here come upon the situation faced by not only the U.S. military but also by all military forces that embark upon operations abroad that do not involve national security. It is often proposed that such a force ought to provide security services to parties who are in legitimate need of it and in whose behalf offering such services would be ethically justified. But is this ethically required?

When we are discussing what ought to be done, in fact the issues are what some agents ought to do. The issue of what ought to be done cannot be divorced from who it is who ought to do what is supposed to be done. For our purposes, then, this means that no official military action is justified unless the duly established military force in question needs to provide security services to the people to whom it has the primary contractual, constitutional responsibility to do so.

For practical purposes, as things stand in our world now, most altercations between nations or countries are, in fact, muddied with histories of misconduct by the people involved on all sides. Even were this not the case, a military force has as its central purpose the duty to stand ready to defend the citizens of the country that it serves. It is no accident that the military is often referred to as the "service."

Inasmuch as embarking on security missions elsewhere would distract from that commitment or involve it in commitments that would conflict with it, then we assume for purposes of this argument that the military is a perfectly legitimate institution that ought not to embark upon interventions abroad.

There are two points to be added to this very brief discussion: Most nations forbid private citizens from embarking on military missions abroad. Yet such a policy could only be justified if such missions are directed against the country itself; otherwise, the policy is morally wrong and should be abandoned. Once the policy is abandoned, the task of going to the aid of foreign causes would no longer need to be laid at the feet of military forces. The nations could enlist the support of citizens who do not have prior military commitments and would not jeopardize them in the effort to lend a hand. Furthermore, preemptive military operations, such as the war contemplated against Iraq, can only be just if there is solid evidence that the target country is preparing to wage war against the country considering such preemptive operations (or against a legitimate ally).

6

LIBERTY: ECONOMIC VERSUS
MORAL BENEFITS

Charges that classical liberalism and libertarianism are amoral or fail to address moral issues adequately are legion. They come from both the left and the right, as well as from various theocratic stances around the globe. One reason for this is that those who level this charge do not recognize prudence as a moral virtue, clearly not as it relates to advancing one's well-being here on Earth. They do not deem this virtue and those related to it, such as industry, ambition, diligence, and thrift, as part of the furniture of a moral or ethical domain. This was explained once beautifully by, of all people, Adam Smith.

> Ancient moral philosophy proposed to investigate wherein consisted the happiness and perfection of a man, considered not only as an individual, but as the member of a family, or a state, and of the great society of mankind. In that philosophy, the duties of human life were treated of as subservient to the happiness and perfection of human life. But, when moral as well as natural philosophy came to be taught only as subservient to theology, the duties of human life were treated of as chiefly subservient to the happiness of a life to come. In the ancient philosophy, the perfection of virtue was represented as necessarily productive to the person who possessed it, of the most perfect happiness in this life. In the modern philosophy, it was frequently represented as almost always inconsistent with any degree of happiness in this life,

and heaven was to be earned by penance and mortification, not by the liberal, generous, and spirited conduct of a man. By far the most important of all the different branches of philosophy became in this manner by far the most corrupted.[1]

When, some time ago, Irving Kristol put his challenge before defenders of human liberty, he seemed to be oblivious to Adam Smith's point. Kristol maintained that those who support the regime of the right to liberty within the realm of community life have not made a case for virtue; they have not demonstrated that their ideal of human political life is in the service of morality, of the good and the common good.[2]

Curiously, this is similar to the charge leveled by Ayn Rand against libertarians who do not embrace her entire philosophy of Objectivism but merely its political implications. She did not appreciate the fact that some people arrive at similar political conclusions via different arguments. Moreover, although these arguments are not good ones, this does not make those who embrace the political principles derived from them unconcerned for those principles.

The challenge implicit in Kristol's own lament is clear: Only to the extent that the free society can be shown to contribute to the good society may it have a claim to moral legitimacy or justice in the broad, ethical sense as distinct from its narrower, political one. This makes good sense. A political order must aim at justice, which is a moral concept applicable to the structure of a polity. Any system indifferent to justice leaves a lot to be desired. This becomes evident in the case of some classical liberals who insist that in time the market will tilt in the direction of what is morally just but that it isn't important that right now it facilitates injustice. For example, some defenders of the marketplace argue that although racial discrimination is morally wrong, market forces will rectify this in time. Those who consider this a matter of justice, however, cannot be satisfied with that reply. They rightly see justice postponed as justice not well served.

Of course, those who care naught for considerations of moral good or evil will simply dismiss Kristol's remarks as orthodox, prescientific, wishful thinking, and even as serious confusion.[3] But those who care naught for such considerations haven't a leg to stand on. Human life is inextricably tied to values, indeed to moral values at that. For human beings, the possibility of choice is real, and the difference between a good and bad one is the difference between doing the moral or the immoral thing.

Morality, in turn, exists because of the fundamental choice that we can make between human life and human death.[4] Of course, there are different accounts of the nature of morality and this isn't the place to deal with all of them. I shall confine myself to considering what Smith above regards as the type of morality in which "the duties of human life were treated of as subservient to the happiness and perfection of human life." In contrast, a Kantian morality is so formalistic that it precludes all references to actual consequences such as happiness or even everlasting salvation. As such, in a basic sense it is irrelevant to living morally!

An ethics that helps us to live makes sense because if we didn't have the threat of early demise facing us, the choices we make wouldn't make much difference. We would continue to live no matter how we choose, so morality would be irrelevant to life and, also, to politics. We would do well at living regardless of our choices if nothing could threaten our lives. If, however, the choices we make are vitally significant for us all, this significance may be what morality involves. I want to argue that in this sense the classical liberal, libertarian polity is intimately related to morality.

The first point to make here is that science, contrary to what much propaganda states, has not demonstrated that man cannot be free.[5] The incorrect belief that it has done so stems from something other than science itself—the philosophers of science, not scientists, are responsible for spreading the false idea that science as such demonstrates humans' passive, reactive, unfree nature.[6] They are wrong—science isn't even in the business of showing such things.[7] Moreover, it has been the imperialism of some of the sciences—physics, chemistry, and, even earlier, mathematics—that made it appear that in studying human nature, human nature itself would have to be what the nature of the subject matter of these fields is: inert.[8]

At any rate, my task here is not to defend the humanities against reductionism. This has been done well by many, among them quite a few scientists, interestingly enough.[9] Even the doctrine of free will is gaining support from scientific minds, some of them in the "hard" sciences such as psychophysics, neurophysiology, and biology.

Instead, I would like to answer Kristol's challenge or at least come near to it. My answer will not argue, however, that the free society is widely defended on moral grounds.[10] Indeed, those supporters of freedom in the classical liberal tradition who are heard from most often in prominent academic and political circles shy away from the moral defense of laissez-faire capitalism and even deny that such a defense is possible and desirable. In contrast, I consider Kristol to be right: Any political system stands or falls intellectually with its capacity, or lack thereof, for the promotion of human virtue. But I will also argue that, despite its infrequent emergence within the forums of academia, there exists a moral defense of political liberty and the corresponding economic system of the free market. Moreover, I will present an argument to show that it is only within a free society that the crucial moral features of human life can be protected and preserved. To that end, I will give some illustrations of what an unfree society must do to these features.

To start off, the economic defense of the free market (mostly advanced by the Chicago School, e.g., Milton Friedman and Yale Brozen) has shown that the bulk of the sound purposes of governmental regulation of human market activities are best achieved in freedom. This means exactly what economists mean when they argue that, considering cost and efficiency, the free market surpasses the regulated economy by leaps and bounds. Economists with even radically varied theoretical frameworks have offered theoretical analyses and historical (empirical) data to support this conclusion. That the free market is most capable of delivering the wants and needs of human beings, including what I would like to distinguish as their most worthy and noble wants and needs, stands undebated.[11] The question concerning economic affairs is not whether freedom is better, but whether better is best. Do economic success, low cost, and high efficiency justify the free society and give intellectual support for the abolition of governmental management?

Before I answer this obviously rhetorical question, I want to point to what will give my response a degree of realism not often found when one hears political ideals discussed. I have in mind the fact that some of the greatest foes of the free market seem clearly to agree with what starts off the economic defense of that system. They agree that regulation has not achieved and is not very likely to achieve the goals set for it. Ralph Nader, someone who does not tire of advocating more and more governmental regulatory activism, agrees with Milton Friedman, for instance. Nader admits that the agencies set up to produce certain valuable results in human economic affairs have failed.[12] Implicitly he is in agreement with the contention that they are most likely to continue to fail—at least if his studies, ranging over hundreds of cases of sloppiness, inefficiency, corruption, injustice, collusion, and other misdeeds of government regulatory bodies, are to be accepted as even partly revelatory.

Despite this basic agreement about the character of government regulation, Naderites continue to call for more of it. What is it that could account for the plausibility of their purpose in the light of this fact?

When I recently proposed these thoughts to a prominent financial journal of free market orientation, one editor said that Nader is a cheap fraud and taking him seriously does him an injustice. I disagree. There may be cheapness and even fraud in some of Nader's and his cohorts' activities, yet that alone will not explain their popularity—a simple evil is not widely tolerated, even when ornamented with moralism and pomposity. It is to insult the electorate seriously and unjustifiably to suggest that all who agree with Nader are cheap frauds—we may as well give up trying to improve the land if that many of us have so little merit.

What is crucial about the Naderite case is that it has a moral defense. Not a morally good one,[13] but one that arises out of a moral point of view, one that advocates and aims to support important human values.[14] One who faults the Naderite mentality should not lose sight of the fact that the announced purposes of the bulk of the Naderites involve serious values. A few of these are truth in advertising, equality of opportunity, ecological balance, product safety, and financial security in old age. As these stand, one must simply admit their value to many of those who live in our country. In broader terms these goals involve what are wisely construed to be noble and morally commendable values, such as the public interest, the national purpose, the moral fiber of society, social justice, and similar general ends. However vaguely these are defined and understood, it is not true that no justifiable moral content could be given to them. When Naderites express righteousness in the process of calling for the attainment, protection, and preservation of these things, they touch on basic moral issues that most people can appreciate to some extent. The broadest term applicable to these goals, the general welfare or common good, is clearly of moral significance in the context of human community life. It is the failure of the economist not to admit to the enormous relevance of these ideals, and Kristol is absolutely on target to lament this fact.[15]

Before I am charged with unfairness, I should consider an objection I have often heard from free market economists. They point out that as economists it is not their business to discuss values, only to show the way to their achievement.[16] Values are everyone's province, and no professional or academic group should feign a monopoly on them. The economists have done well with their arguments in behalf of liberty—are their data from history and their theoretical analyses not exactly what will show rational people what goals are attainable and how well by way of governmental regulation? Having done this, they can only hope that people will learn the lesson. Once it is learned, only the foolish or fraudulent will persist.

Two points about these objections. First, most economists[17] do not just decline the invitation and temptation to endorse moral values—they deny that these *can be known* by anyone.[18] They are right to hold values to be the province of all individuals, but they are wrong to hold that none can identify moral values with success. This is an epistemological proclamation and the province of philosophy. To the extent that economists rule out the prospect of objective value judgments, they are being intellectual imperialists, just as philosophers would be by announcing that their work invalidates the market analysis or historical studies of economists. (The division of labor applies in scholarship also.)

The other point to be made is that cost/efficiency analysis simply is not adequate to show that politicians should not regulate economic activity. Admittedly, such regulation does worse for its purposes than what free markets have done—plenty of studies demonstrate this fact—but more is needed to demonstrate what should or should not be done. Without such a demonstration, advocates of regulation can argue as follows: The values sought after are very important, and very important goals require high risk; so, despite the high risk of failure, measures that have not worked in the majority of cases must be employed to try to secure those goals. I like to use the analogy of the drowning child to illustrate the point of this argument. Should a parent see his or her child in distress or grave danger, and should the prospects of rescuing the child be virtually nil, the parent is still entirely justified, even duty-bound, to make the effort. Cost and efficiency are hardly factors to be introduced. If one could know for certain that nothing good and only harm can come from the attempt, then it might be good advice to discourage the effort, but great values that may or may not be achieved should be pursued unless we know that success is impossible.

The argument of Naderites has this implicit structure. The goals desired are widely admitted for good reason. Clearly poverty exists, dishonesty can be found in most professions and businesses, and so on—to deny these facts is futile. The claim that on the whole we can do better in freedom is not relevant when the only factors cited in defense of freedom are economic ones. People already tend to give lip service to altruism in their moralizing moments, so how could they resist Nader & Co. when all they ask is that private gain, wealth, insistence on efficiency, and the like be given up for the often slight but undeniably worthy chance of attaining what is good? From ignorance or whatever reason, the public has the inclination to view the economic case with suspicion. Is it not callous to suggest that for wealth and efficiency we ought to abandon massive efforts to help people? Are we so cheap? The moralists have all the arguments on their side.

Moreover, the economist of the empiricist variety,[19] who relies on historical studies alone to point up the inefficiency and high cost of government regulation, cannot counter Nader's call for better people and his promise of greater virtue in the future. From the past, we may have learned how to avoid failures (at least, we should have), and empiricists are impotent to argue against this since they can tell us only about what happened and perhaps what may or is likely to happen. Yet surely with perseverance people can overcome the limitations of the past. That at least is something plausible. However cheap and fraudulent the promises are, the idea is not necessarily wrong. There are, after we have considered these issues honestly, some people who have been helped by regulation, some people who a thoroughly mismanaged social security program has helped, some who were told the truth by businessmen only after the state threatened legal action, and some mothers who might have bought an unsafe toy had it not been for the government's edict. The list could go on. Although the losses suffered from the high cost and inefficiency of the government's regulatory activities is only known by a "what might have been" analysis, the achievements of the state are carefully recorded. (We need only note how rapidly reports of severe losses emerged after Richard Nixon discontinued certain welfare-type programs. No one mentioned that by taking less from the taxpayer, or by not taking more than would have been necessary otherwise, people could achieve goals not open to them before.)

In the end, the Naderite mentality has the greater, more realistic appeal to the public. Government must act, even if at great cost and with little success, because the values lost from inaction come to losses we cannot tolerate, to moral neglect, callousness, and cruelty all for the sake of economic welfare. Unless a better case can be made for liberty, its opponents will carry the day. If no such case can be given, then they ought to. There are greater goods than economic welfare, riches, smooth production, efficient exchange, and effective distribution, the "virtues" of the free market.

From the above conclusion, I propose to move on to more positive points. I want to argue, in answer to Kristol and in opposition to the Naderites, that pursuing the regulatory road has worse than economically bad consequences.

First of all, economic liberty, as religious, press, or artistic liberty, is a species of political liberty. Without this liberty, the moral life itself is impossible, and that life carries into economics. Liberty ensures the possibility of choice. H. B. Acton put it rather mildly when he said: "Competitive markets are likely to do less harm than centralized economic planning and to give more scope for intellectual and moral excellence." He adds that "a centrally planned economy is bound to monopolize ideas and even to ration them, whereas in a society where competitive markets prevail it is not only trade, but also thoughts and men that are free."[20]

If these observations are correct, it would appear that liberty, defined as the absence of government regulation, is at least a prerequisite for the moral life. Not very long ago, the Supreme Court of the United States seemed to be echoing Acton's remarks—perhaps somewhat uncharacteristically, what with its recent rulings on censorship[21]—when it said:

The right to enjoy property without unlawful deprivation, no less than the right to speak or the right to travel, is in truth a "personal" right, whether the "property" in question be a welfare check, a home, or a savings account. In fact, a fundamental interdependence exists between the personal right to liberty and the personal right to property. Neither could have any meaning without the other. That rights in property are basic civil rights has long been recognized.[22]

Aside from this conceptual or logical relationship between economic freedom (property rights) and the liberty to act in general, we can point to other possible values that may be put over against the value of pursuing the general welfare via government regulation. Although these cannot be argued for here, I should think that those I have in mind are as clear-cut as any mentioned in the earlier list of values sought after by way of regulation.

Consider, for example, that when businesses and individuals are regulated, they are frequently ordered to act in ways that will impose upon them serious costs and deprive them of the opportunity to choose from other alternatives. Thus, governmental inspections impose upon firms serious expenses and limitations of choice. But *in justice,* a person or a group of persons should not have to suffer a loss of wealth or liberty unless they have committed some wrong. The imposition of such costs is exactly like the imposition of punishment upon someone who has been found guilty of a crime. Just for entering a profession or enterprise, a person or group *must* suffer these penalties that are the direct consequence of governmental regulation.

In addition, the simple fact that some business activity *might* harm someone has been thought to justify the imposition of such costs. From the prohibition of cigarette commercials, to the limitation of sex and violence in television programming, to the limitation of vitamin dosage—all these goals are pursued with only the following justification (offered, in this instance, by former New York Senator Jacob Javits): "While we protect the right of the individual to buy vitamins, we must at the same time safeguard him and those individuals who may not be aware of the dangers of potential over-use of vitamins against the possible hazards."[23] In short, the *potential* overuse, the *possible* hazards, and the fact that some individuals *may* not be aware supposedly justify the loss of people's liberty imposed, in this case, by the FDA.

The principle that is violated by these measures would appear to be as clear as any could be. We are generally aware of the significance of having to prove the guilt of someone before being justified in imposing penalties upon her. This is a principle of justice. Yet this principle is violated to an immeasurable extent in the case of the imposition of penalties upon people *who have done nothing wrong to anyone,* who have injured no one, who have shown no intent of injuring anyone—in short, who are guilty of nothing. In line with the case offered by Senator Javits, *any* individual could be incarcerated, since any person *might* be a criminal, each of us *may* not be aware of what we ought to do, and each of us is a potential hazard since we all *could* choose to harm people, ignore the law, and become careless so that we would pose a hazard. In fact, the same argument that Senator Javits used to justify the regulation of vitamin production can be used to justify the regulation of the content of books, movies, television shows, and newspapers. As a famous television research project into the possible relationship between programs containing violent scenes and children viewing them concluded:

> For some children, under some conditions, some television is harmful. For other children under the same conditions, or for the same children under other conditions, it may be beneficial. For most children under most conditions most television is probably neither particularly harmful nor particularly beneficial.[24]

As everyone knows, thousands of people are calling upon the Federal Communications Commission (FCC) to stop violence on television. That means that they are asking the government to force networks, actors, writers, camera crews, and others to suffer losses and to forgo the freedom to act in accordance with judgments made voluntarily. That this violates the principle that a person is innocent unless *proved* guilty (and thus should not suffer the conditions that are due a guilty individual) is clear. If it can be shown, as I think it can, that government regulation violates that principle, then the *moral* case against such regulation would surely be stronger than the Chicago School's arguments make it appear.

The principle of "equal protection under the law," which is itself a derivation from the moral principle that each human being is equally endowed with rights that ought to be protected and preserved, is also violated by regulatory measures. By prohibiting some people's pursuit of *their* goals (i.e., by diverting their incomes and labors into projects they *personally* cannot choose) while enabling others to decide what such incomes and labors ought to support, the principle of the equality of all citizens is violated. That Werner von Braun, for example, could have his goals incorporated into public policy, that Ralph Nader could have his projects financed by monies collected from others who are not given a choice about the matter—these and, of course, millions of other cases constitute a violation of the principle of equality. In short, it is morally right that each person's goals in life be regarded as immune from interference (this automatically excludes such "goals" as murder and theft since *these cannot be pursued without violating the principle itself*). When some actions, including governmental regulation of economic affairs, conflict with that principle, then they ought not to be undertaken. Thus another moral value is undermined in the pursuit of values by means of governmental regulation. That is to say, pursuing the values of the general welfare (e.g., space flights, which could certainly be admitted to be worthwhile pursuits of many individuals) by means of violating the principles of equality and justice (i.e., via government regulation) is unjustifiable.

Finally, I would like to point to yet another moral objection to government regulation. When the responsibility to make decisions about the conduct of those who are regulated

is left with the officials of the government, the moral autonomy of the latter is undermined. When people are forced to
conduct themselves in one way, their liberty to choose what
kind of life they will lead is destroyed. This, in effect, is the
same moral fault of governmental regulation I pointed to
first, only this time it emerges in the context of more concrete considerations. Here I want to focus on the fact that
governmental regulation leads to a discernible dissolution of
two distinguishable but inseparable features of morally significant conduct, judgment and behavior. When the decision as
to what will be done is left to others, the person's own judgment ceases to have a serious bearing upon his behavior. Fear
of enforcement remains the motive for action for at least the
economic segments of a person's life. This approach to the relationship between government and the citizens is best characterized by the term "paternalism." In the case of parents
vis-à-vis children, it is justifiable for a father to make at least
some of the decisions about a child's conduct. After all, here
we are concerned with children. In the realm of government
regulation it is an entirely different matter. Some human beings, *as such,* prevent other human beings, *as such,* from making decisions in the conduct of *their* lives. It does not require
expert training in psychology to draw the inference that this
leads to moral disorientation, to the gradual loss of a mature
moral perspective on one's life. In the end, moral choices as
such are more and more difficult to identify and only fear of
"the law" becomes significant. (I must admit that here I am
thinking of the moral elements within recent governmental
scandals, but the point applies generally, even if it is the result
of philosophical speculation and not controlled empirical research.)

Although members of the Chicago School, especially
Milton Friedman, are well aware of the above considerations,
because of their commitment to economics as an empirical
science and the subjectivist, skeptical tradition in moral philosophy, they cannot raise them in opposition to governmental regulation. Because the Nader groups eschew scientific

purity and pride themselves on being "activists," they can focus upon the values that have always been pursued—at least in the rhetoric of their inception—by way of government regulation. Finding no powerful *moral* opposition, the Nader group enjoys considerably more vigorous moral support than could the Chicago group. Politics is, after all, a moral enterprise.

Yet the Chicago group's efforts are *indispensable* to making any kind of a moral case against government regulation. For if we did not know that means other than state action are available for improving on the activities of economic agents—many of whom are clearly engaged in shoddy practices—the case against paternalistic state action would be very difficult to make. (One need but take a cursory glance at TV commercials, examine one's recently purchased appliances, or research the nutritional content of some foods.) Moreover, it is important, though clearly not decisive, to learn that governments are unable to force the people to protect themselves and to keep their voluntary interactions free of trouble. It lends strength to the moral argument in demonstrating, by reference to well-scrutinized history, that morality and prudence really do go together, that it is indeed better to be good, even in political affairs, than to be bad. In short, a morally good system can be good for human life.

Unfortunately, in their effort to be convincing about their scientific purity, many members of the Chicago School go further than simply abstaining from infusing their scholarly work with value judgments. They have been known to announce that value judgments are unsupportable[25] and that they are simply tastes or preferences, entirely arbitrary and unjustifiable. Perhaps, as with other defenders of human liberty and the free society, these individuals believe that (1) laying claim to knowledge of moral principles will serve to antagonize other, scientifically minded individuals; and (2) if no one can know what is right and wrong in human conduct, in even the most general sense of moral principles, then everyone has a good case for preventing the imposition of such beliefs on himself. If we *know* another is sinning, however, we must stop him.

In fact, it never follows from simply knowing what ought to be done by someone that another should force her to comply.[26] It is only by a rational demonstration of the fact that such enforcement is itself morally justified that it may be undertaken, a principle upon which a good portion of our criminal law rests. So moral skepticism serves neither a strategic nor a moral function, since, regarding the latter, it does not avail one of the moral justification to *resist* aggression upon herself. In other words, by refusing to approach the issue of government regulation from a moral point of view, reinforced as it must always be, by sound economic analysis, the members of the Chicago School have robbed themselves of the logical right to advocate a course of action they have, in fact, suggested in many of their studies. They have disabled themselves in respect to making the best possible case for human liberty within the realm of economics as well as within any other realm of human conduct. They have, at least in their position as professionals, lost to Nader's Raiders the argument concerning whether government regulation of the economy should be abandoned or carried out, despite repeated failures, high cost, and inefficiency in the hope of at least some morally worthwhile achievements that such activity promises. It seems clear to me that they could have made a far stronger case by admitting that the dispute is, after all, a moral and political one and only secondarily one involving economics.

Kristol notes that, despite the attack upon scientism by such eminent free market defenders as F. A. Hayek, they have to "fall back on a faith in the ultimate benefits of 'self-realization'—a phrase [Hayek] uses as infrequently as possible, but which he is nevertheless forced to use at crucial instances."[27] Kristol is quite correct when he asks, "And what if the 'self' that is 'realized' under the conditions of liberal capitalism is a self that despises liberal capitalism, and uses its liberty to subvert and abolish a free society? To this question, Hayek—like Friedman—has no answer."[28]

Yet it is unclear that anyone can have a *final* answer to the question. From the point of view of someone who accepts the nature of man as a moral agent, it is impossible to *guarantee* against human corruption in or outside the free society. What seems clear, however, is that in a free society the likelihood of individual moral excellence is greater if for no other reason than because each person can make the effort to achieve that excellence.

But it is entirely unjust to charge the free society with some fault for not managing to guarantee against human failure, even against the collapse of a politically noble system. Kristol may imagine that imposing stringent rules upon a society will do that trick, but dictatorships simply *cannot* be beneficial in these (or other) ways. Nothing on the order of a good human community is possible when people who think themselves morally superior begin to play parents to their fellows. A restrained, maybe even well-behaved, Skinnerian human community is at least imaginable under those conditions—but not a morally and politically excellent one.

I want to close this discussion with the remarks of Leo Strauss. In his outstanding book *Natural Right and History*,[29] which often chides liberal American politics on grounds alluded to by Kristol,[30] Strauss gave the following rendition of the Greek or classical conception of liberty, one he seemed certainly to have emulated in his own discussions of political affairs. Strauss wrote that

> political freedom, and especially that political freedom that justifies itself by the pursuit of human excellence, is not a gift of heaven; it becomes actual only through the efforts of many generations, and its preservation always requires the highest degree of vigilance.[31]

It may be that some defenders of liberty fail to give it the best support by their refusal to acknowledge that the pursuit of human excellence requires it. When we notice this, however, our response cannot be to turn away from liberty. It must be to reiterate the most effective defense for it: Only a free human being can aspire to moral excellence, and everyone, whoever he is and however possible it is that he will not so aspire, has the right to the condition that makes this aspiration a real possibility.

7

AGAINST UTILITARIANISM

One of the important questions that arise in connection with political economy is how to reason about public policies. When citizens consider how problems are to be solved, they can think in several different ways, but two are prominent and have been the most widely considered live options, at least in Western societies. These are the utilitarian and the rights-based approaches to forging public policies.

Utilitarianism, a form of consequentialism, is the theory of values that urges us to do what will produce the greatest good, as measured by what most people want or desire, or by what will satisfy most of them. For example, whether farmers should receive government subsidies in the form of, say, price supports, is often considered on the basis of whether this will have over-all good or bad social results.

The rights-based approach sets certain principles—for example, unalienable rights—as guides to public policies. For example, whether women should be protected from rapists or even stalkers is usually considered on the basis of what their rights are, not whether such protection will have overall social benefits as compared with the cost of providing it.

In America, as well as in other relatively open societies, there is much debate about whether to respect individual rights regardless of currently estimated consequences, or to ignore those rights if the consequences are deemed to be worth it.

The founding documents of America, and the broad intellectual tradition of classical liberalism from which those documents emerged, consider both the general welfare and our unalienable rights. (Adam Smith was a type of utilitarian, whereas John Locke was a rights theorist.) Not that these two concerns must be in conflict: Often, the best results society-wide do come from acting in a principled fashion. But those who champion utilitarianism tend to believe not in principles but in consequences alone, whereas rights theorists tend to put the primary emphasis on principles.

GUN CONTROL AND SOFTWARE CONTROL

For example, in the ongoing debate about gun control or the more recent dispute about whether Microsoft Corporation ought to be broken up, even those who hold the same opinion about what ought to be done do not defend that opinion the same way. Opponents of gun control sometimes say that such measures are too costly and do not produce enough good, so scrap them; others say that people have the right to bear arms, so no one has the authority to ban or regulate gun ownership whatever the estimated consequences. With regard to the antitrust suit against Microsoft, some argue that breaking up Microsoft will hurt more people than it will help, so it is a bad idea; others say that Microsoft has a right to conduct business as long as it does not engage in force and fraud, and that it hasn't done these, so don't break it up and never mind how the public will fare from this.

Different arguments, same conclusion. So, if we're getting to the same place, why even bother asking whether the rights-based approach or the utilitarian approach is the correct one?

Well, for someone who cares about the character of politics, not to mention the successful living of life, the issue is crucial. Can principles be identified to the extent that we can stick to them confidently in every context to which they properly apply—or must we consider each case anew, from scratch? Is it not enough to know that we have basic rights as human beings deriving from our very nature and the requirements of our survival, and then to abide by this knowledge, whether or not *some* of the consequences of respecting those rights turn out to be inconvenient to somebody? Or must our individual rights be held hostage to a demonstration of the wider public benefits each time the question comes up, with those rights regarded as expendable if the tally of public benefits looms sufficiently large?

The latter is clearly not a calculation we make when it comes to freedom of expression and religion. We do not try to determine in each case whether the freedom to worship leads to a better religious climate, or whether freedom of expression, especially in the press, produces more good than, say, a government-regulated press. Why? *Because we care about those freedoms so much*—and so we want each individual to enjoy them as a matter of course. We don't want to put those freedoms at risk by letting them be subject to a cost-benefit analysis every time someone publishes a broadside or opens a church. Presumably we have learned that lesson a long time ago and we take it that this lesson has staying power. Of course, our allegiance to principle even in these realms is not perfect—witness the speech constraints that the U.S. government imposes on broadcasters but does not impose on print publishers.

Rights theorists think that the same principled approach is valid when it comes to other arenas, including the right to bear arms. Sure, some people will misuse guns and this will have some undesirable, even deadly, consequences. All in all, however, respecting the rights of individuals to bear arms also ought to be seen as having staying power, as an expression of the right of self-defense that is in turn based on the right to life itself. To consistently respect and protect basic individual rights is the best overall course for human beings to take as they live in their communities.

JUST A LOT OF FLUX?

Some see this approach as mistaken because they believe that the world is not a steady, stable place at all but rather in constant flux, so that no such principles can be counted on. Even if principles do hold up over time when it comes to scientific realms like physics and chemistry, the same cannot be said of human affairs.

If principles do not apply in human affairs, to insist that people be honest or generous or just as a matter of principle, rather than on a pragmatic case-by-case basis, makes no sense. We should not even praise integrity, the virtue of upholding one's basic ethical principles in the face of even the greatest of temptations. Keeping promises and honoring oaths, too—even when inconvenient—would be silly. No such consistency could be expected of sensible people. There would certainly be no grounds for assailing, say, the kind of near-continuous lying and promise-breaking we have come to expect from the likes of former U.S. President Bill Clinton.

However, the utilitarian approach to public policy has its critics. There are many who point out that if there are no reliable principles, then calculating the consequences of policies is an impossible and unintelligible endeavor. If there is no rhyme or reason to human life, then all such consequentialist calculations are themselves pointless. Why should we think that breaking up Microsoft is going to be bad for the economy just because similar break-ups have been bad in the past? If, however, there is something we can *learn* from the past, it also follows that we could have learned that, in general, government should not interfere with people's economic affairs. That would imply that we should respect individual rights as a matter of principle.

Prominent libertarian David Boaz, editor of *The Libertarian Reader,* comments on the matter in an interview in the publication *Full Context:*

> There may be a sense among some Objectivists and other libertarians motivated primarily by concern for individual

rights that it's a happy coincidence that pursuing a policy of individual rights leads to the results of prosperity and social harmony, but that if you had to choose, you would choose individual rights over good consequences. That's a false dichotomy. It is implicit, although perhaps not played up as much as it should have been in [Ayn] Rand's work, that it is not a happy coincidence—it would be unreasonable to expect that the proper philosophy for man did not lead to good results. It would make no sense to demand individual rights for a species for whom the pursuit of individual rights would result in social conflict and poverty. These two lines of argument have to work together.

Of course, most rights theorists such as Ayn Rand and the neo-Objectivists in whose ranks I belong are in some sense consequentialists (or, more precisely, teleologists)! Rights are vital so that we can choose—so that we have the opportunity to choose what is right (while unavoidably running the risk of choosing what is wrong). To the extent that individual rights are protected, every particular individual enjoys the good consequence of being free to act on his own behalf; further good consequences (for himself and others) then depend on how he chooses to act.

The reason for the "happy coincidence" that respecting rights generates social harmony and prosperity is that when rights are respected, the incentive structure is such that doing wrong tends to hurt oneself, mostly, and the results may not be simply dumped on others. At the same time, one has all the incentive in the world to do productive and beneficial things that are good for others as well as oneself. But there is no guarantee that protecting individual rights will produce, in any given instance, more goodies than some kind of politically coerced or regulated labor might. So when the consequentialists appear to offer such guarantees, they run the serious risk—historically well documented—that if just once they cannot deliver on the promises, argumentatively they will become vulnerable.

Laissez-faire, in short, is no panacea when it comes to secondary consequences—only the best bet!

HONESTY IS THE BEST POLICY

All in all, then, I support the principled or rights-based approach. In normal contexts, honesty is the best policy, even if at times it does not achieve the desired good results; so is respect for every individual's rights to life, liberty, and property. All in all, this is what will ensure the best consequences—in the long run and as a rule.

Therefore, one need not be very concerned about the most recent estimate of the consequences of banning or not banning guns, breaking up or not breaking up Microsoft, or any other public policy, for that matter. It is enough to know that violating the rights of individuals to bear arms is a bad idea, and that history and analysis support our understanding of principle. To violate rights has always produced greater damage than good, so let's not do it, even when we are terribly tempted to do so. Let's not do it precisely because to do so would violate the fundamental requirements of human nature. It is those requirements that should be our guide, not some recent empirical data that have no staying power (according to their very own theoretical terms).

Finally, you will ask, isn't this being dogmatic? Haven't we learned not to bank too much on what we've learned so far, when we also know that learning can always be improved, modified, even revised? Isn't progress in the sciences and technology proof that past knowledge always gets overthrown a bit later?

As in science and engineering, so in morality and politics: We must go with what we know but be open to change—provided that the change is warranted. Simply because some additional gun controls or regulations might save lives (*some* lives, perhaps at the expense of other lives) and simply because breaking up Microsoft might improve the satisfaction of consumers (*some* consumers, perhaps at the expense of the satisfaction of other consumers) are no reasons to violate basic rights. Only if and when there are solid, demonstrable reasons to do so should we throw out the old principles and bring on the new principles. Any such reasons would have to speak to the same level of fundamentality and relevance as that incorporated by the theory of individual rights itself.

Those defending consequentialism, like Justice Oliver Wendell Holmes, have argued the opposite thesis: Unless one can prove, beyond a doubt, that violating rights in a particular instance is necessarily wrong in the eyes of a "rational and fair man," the state may go ahead and "accept the natural outcome of dominant opinion" and violate those rights.[1]

Such is now the leading jurisprudence of the United States, a country that inaugurated its political life by declaring to the world that each of us possesses *unalienable* rights, ones that may never be violated no matter what!

8

REFLECTIONS ON THE RIGHT
TO PRIVATE PROPERTY

WHY *PRIVATE* PROPERTY?

Let me begin by explaining what I mean by the right to private property and why I use what some now consider an old-fashioned term rather than, say, "the right to several property."[1] The right to private property is the social-political principle that adult human beings may not be prohibited or prevented by anyone from acquiring, holding, and trading (with willing parties) valued items not already owned by others. Such a right is, thus, unalienable and, if in fact justified, should enjoy respect and legal protection in a just human community.[2] One reason that it is useful, at least in the context of political philosophy and moral theory, to keep the wording "the right to private property" is that it more clearly connotes an important element of classic liberal thought—namely, individualism.

With the development of classical liberalism, there emerged in Western political thought a shift of perspective with regard to what constitutes the primary value in social-political matters. Classical liberalism saw not the group—for example, a tribe, class, state, or nation—as paramount, but the human individual. Political efforts to implement the new viewpoint entailed the gradual transferring of power from a few or even one person as the source of collective authority and power to more and more segments of society. This dispersal of power generated clear social gains, for when individuals are regarded as sovereign and particular persons tend to possess much more diffused and diversified power, they are much less likely to coercively impose themselves on others by, say, starting a war, even when they disagree very seriously. When implemented via law and public policy, individualism is thus much more conducive to peace and, as a result, to prosperity than is any form of collectivism.

It was also clear to the classical liberals that economic productivity owed much to the "invisible hand" of market processes—the kind of activity that takes place when the visible hand of government confines itself to *protecting* terms of contract rather than *dictating* those terms. The liberal order gained further support from the conflict between church and state, of course; here again, too, the goal of decentralizing power was a major if indirect factor in how the conflict played out.

From the beginning, then, classical liberalism enjoyed considerable support on practical grounds—the ability of a classical liberal order to help people attain various widely sought-after objectives. But why would these practical consequences flow from establishing liberal institutions? Why is it better to have a more decentralized polity, an unplanned economy? Why would prosperity come more readily from the invisible rather than the visible hand? Moreover, if the liberal order does achieve all these real-world benefits, why did it come under increasing intellectual assault? Why was it *vulnerable* to that assault?

The plain fact is that as far as its ethical presuppositions and implications are concerned, individualism and, in consequence, classical liberalism have not fared all that well. These views have constantly been charged with being inimical to community life and human fellowship, spawning hedonism and materialism, and so forth. Wrongheaded these criticisms may well be, but without a solid moral case it is difficult to show this. One reason for this is that morality is extremely important in human affairs. Most people do not confidently embrace a political stance, much less fight for it, unless it embraces certain basic moral principles—unless it falls within the compass of a moral vision that makes sense and is even inspiring. Concerns about practicality as such thus never suffice to persuade people of the soundness of political systems and public policies.

It is part of the point of this chapter to show that private property rights accord with certain basic moral principles. I will argue that human agency is indispensable to any sensible moral framework and treat particularly the example of the moral virtue of prudence. I will argue that individualism embraces these principles and that the right to private property makes their actual realization possible in human community life. The collectivist critics of individualism neglect such principles because they misconstrue or ignore the actual nature of the individual and, thus, the individual's proper relationship to society.

SOCIETY AS ORGANISM

The idea that we are all mere parts of a large human organism has gained a very strong intellectual standing in our time. A great many people make reference to humanity—as when they talk about sacrificing oneself, one's private interests, or one's materialistic goals for humanity. Others refer to smaller groups—for instance, the community, ethnic group, or race—as the organisms of significance.

It's almost a feature of mainstream thought to consider each of us not primarily as individuals but only as parts of some larger whole: "Don't you have something more important to live for than yourself?" or, "Isn't there something greater than yourself to which your life must be devoted for it to be worthwhile?" are common examples. Less loosely, some thinkers, such as the philosopher Charles Taylor, argue that we all *belong* to a group by dint of our very humanity, our very nature as human beings. He tells us,

> Theories which assert the primacy of rights are those which take as the fundamental, or at least a fundamental, principle

of their political theory the ascription of certain rights to individuals which deny the same status to a principle of belonging or obligation, that is a principle which states our obligation as men to belong to or sustain society, or a society of a certain type, or to obey authority or an authority of a certain type.[3]

Never mind that Taylor cannot supply us with any such theories—as did John Locke, for example, when he rested basic human rights on ethics or natural law. What is important for Taylor is that if you live only to make the most of *your* life, you're not really living a *significant enough* life. A significant life must fulfill a greater purpose. Humanity's purpose (whatever that may be) is one of the candidates. God's purpose (whatever that may be) is another candidate. Ecologists have a biological purpose in mind. But a significant life "belongs" to (is an ineluctable part of) the effort to pursue this purpose; thus our lives, to be properly significant, may be subordinated, by force if need be, to such purposes.[4] If we don't choose such significance ourselves, it is to be chosen for us, and no principle of "individual rights" can be played as a trump card to bar the imposition.

There's a very prominent tradition in political thought of selecting alternative wholes larger than ourselves as the proposed beneficiaries of significant human actions. This can lead to forcing individuals to be used for purposes to which they do not consent. Once it is accepted that human individuals are merely parts of a larger whole (as if members of a partnership or team), they have enforceable obligations to the goals of that large whole. They belong to it. They owe it something. After all, if the individual's own personal values, goals, and selfish "preferences" are paramount to her only *as an individual,* but she *as an individual* is not the proper ultimate beneficiary of her own actions, it is only appropriate to thwart her personal goal-seeking and enlist her in the service of that which *is* regarded as the proper ultimate beneficiary—whether God or group.

To appreciate the appeal of the idea that society as a whole is equivalent to an organism, consider how in certain cases we treat such wholes as our individual selves. If something happens to an ear, for example, and yet we prize our appearance with ear intact, we don't hesitate to confiscate tissue from a part of the body that is not so visible in order to repair the ear; the late Irish actor Richard Harris, whose nose was destroyed in a fight, allowed doctors to replace it with part of his hip bone. We think it is proper to sacrifice a less critical part of the body to the needs of the self as a whole, the organism as a whole.

Well, if humanity is a yet larger organism, then maybe a given individual/cell is not quite as important a part of it as another is. For the sake of the greater organism, the less important individual can be sacrificed for the more important individual (or the goals of the less important one can be sacrificed for those of the more important one). One person may be equivalent to an eye and the other to just a useless thumb. This picture is widely embraced because of the belief that humanity is some organic whole.

SOCIALISM AND HUMANITY

Now consider that one of the interesting aspects of socialism is that in deep-seated socialist theory *there are no individuals.* Marx said it directly: "The human essence is the true collectivity of man."[5] He believed that human beings constitute species-beings and comprise "an organic whole" in the collectivity we call humanity.[6] For a consistent, thoroughgoing socialist, what is important about you and me is that we belong to the human race, somewhat analogously to the way a bee belongs to its hive or an ant to its colony—except that in this case, the constituent parts are intelligent persons. According to such a view, individuality is not merely secondary; it is virtually extinguished.

This is especially true of international socialism, but National Socialism (i.e., that of the Nazi Party) and even more restrictive, local forms of socialism also emphasize the group as a whole and *its* alleged plan, telos, or destiny. Even communitarians, as vague as their conception of a community may be (so that one cannot quite pin them down as socialists given the leeway they provide for some elements of individualism), speak in terms of "us" and "we" when designating the primarily valued party in discussions of public policy. By this view, too, then, the individual can at times be sacrificed if some putative gains can be thereby attained for the group, collective, or community.

INDIVIDUALISM AND HISTORICISM

One of the most prominent and oft-repeated criticisms leveled at classical liberalism, especially by students of various brands of Marxism—there are about 300 versions floating around now—is that the whole classical liberal emphasis on individuality is a kind of a historical glitch: a temporary phase that played a useful historical role but now can and should be dispensed with. To evoke classical liberal notions in modern times is thus to reveal one's ideas (and maybe one's self as well) as antiquated and irrelevant.

The Marxists and many others (some who echo the Marxist line without realizing it) claim that in the sixteenth century the individual was *invented,* not merely discovered, or his existence was politically affirmed, for the sake of sustaining economic productivity. In order to motivate wealth creation, the individual had to be made to seem significant. That significance is a myth, but a useful myth (useful at one time in history, at any rate). It's like telling a plain woman that she is beautiful so that she will do something for you. What she does is still of benefit even if her beauty is a myth. Similarly, say Marxists, there was a period of human history during which the belief in the importance of the individual had an objective historical function: not because the belief is true, but because it contributed to certain crucial elements of capitalism.

History, by this view, is the record of the growth of humanity from infancy to full maturity. Tribalism would be the first stage and communism the final stage. Marx regarded the

Greek era as the childhood of humanity. The bourgeois epoch might be its adolescence. Adolescents embark upon all sorts of useless ventures, such as getting up at 4:00 A.M. to drive someplace—not because there's something important to do there (although they may kid themselves into believing so) but really as a sort of unwitting exercise to prepare for adulthood. The otherwise pointless excursions of adolescence serve as training for the eventual serious challenges of maturity. Some ecologists look at history this way, as do many of those moral visionaries who consider humanity to be one big family or other kind of collectivity.

When one considers humanity this way, as an organism unto itself that is steadily ascending various historical stages, individualism can be regarded as one of these stages—a necessary stage, but certainly not the final one. From a Marxist or collectivist perspective, the admission that there was indeed such a "stage" of history and even that it had some passing utility allows one to accommodate a fair amount of unavoidable historical data, while also feeling justified in relegating that stage to the dustheap. One can then dismiss any contemporary individualist or classical liberal claims as irrelevant to the current progress of history, without troubling oneself overmuch about any arguments for or against them.

INDIVIDUALISM AS A LIVE OPTION

If one recognizes collectivism as a misguided view of human life, one must carefully and effectively argue in response to these well-developed and often honestly and sincerely meant doctrines. One must demonstrate that it is indeed individuals who count for the most in the world. One must prove, widespread opinion to the contrary notwithstanding, that concepts like "individual rights" are universal in their applicability and not relevant only to some limited historical epoch.

Collectivist arguments must be answered because they are plausible (at least within the confines of their own assumptions) and exert enormous influence in the world intellectual community. The story they rely upon may be false, but in order to cope with it, one must get to the heart of the actual situation and demonstrate beyond all reasonable doubt that the true story is a different one. One must show that one's own understanding of what's going on is more rational, coherent, comprehensive, and explanatory. Otherwise the deceptive story will be the only persuasive account making the rounds.

Unless liberalism is able to identify a better story than that advanced by champions of the organic view of humanity, liberalism will be defeated, at least theoretically. And although theoretical defeat isn't always decisive, it certainly impairs the confidence with which a position can be supported and put into practice.

So we need to answer the question: What is morally right about the institution of private property rights? Why it is justifiable to have such laws in a community? By this I do not mean such instrumental or pragmatic matters as the utility of property rights law for purposes of facilitating productivity, wealth, or innovation. It may be all that, of course. But such considerations do not address the more crucial issue of whether private property makes good sense morally—or should be condemned for promoting hedonism, selfishness, and greed, as many critics would insist.

MORALITY, HUMANITY, AND INDIVIDUALITY

Morality concerns how to live one's life properly, rightly, in a worthy manner, nobly, and honorably. To be morally good is to choose to do what will make a person excellent as the kind of being he is, and thereby survive and flourish as that kind of being. That means choosing to live in accordance with certain virtues—such as honesty, prudence, generosity, and courage.

Since living a morally good life means striving to fulfill the requirements of one's nature, our first task will be to take a brief look at human nature.

Aristotle spelled out explicitly what makes us distinctively human: a self-awareness that consists of thinking; of understanding in concepts; and of guiding our conduct by principles, not just by range-of-the moment feelings, wishes, or desires. The human capacity to reason is so widely evident in human life and history that, although philosophers like to discuss the nuances, no one can sensibly doubt it. What is less widely acknowledged is that human nature also includes, as one of its distinctive features, a significant element of individuality. This is vital, because private property rights tie in very closely with human individuality.

The sheer fact of individuality is well nigh inescapable. If one imagines that a good friend has died, it is plainly nonsense to believe, "Oh well, I'll just replace my friend with someone else." One cannot simply replace a person with another if one regards her as she is most basically—as a unique individual whom one has come to know specifically, not just as a member of a class of people, such as dentists or auto mechanics.

Pets can also take on this individual significance to an extent, insofar as we tend to anthropomorphize them. On the other hand, replacing a cow, fly, rock, and most other things in the world is no problem in one sense, in that they aren't important to us *individually*; we don't suffer the trauma of losing a unique individual. Such items are unique, in fact, but we generally don't *care* about their uniqueness as such. They are important to us with respect to their relationship to other things, whereas in the case of human beings it is everyone's individuality that matters most, especially in those most significant personal or intimate relationships. You fall in love with an individual as a particular individual, not as a banker— when you really fall in love, that is. Some people "fall in love" with a type, true enough, but there's something perverse about that. It is sad to hear, "Well, I love him" because "he's in uniform" or "has a big car."

Clearly there is something irreducibly, inescapably individual about everybody. Just think about yourself. How do you want to be regarded by friends and others close to you? As a student? As an American or Rumanian or Hispanic? Or as a woman or basketball player? Is there not in fact something unique that captures who *you* are, and that you want others to see and respond to? As the character of John Quincy Adams put it in the movie *Amistad,* to come to know a person one must ask not *what* someone is but *who* someone is. Your deepest *identity* isn't racial, ethnic, religious, or even professional. It is individual.

Our individual identities are also, in large part, self-chosen. In intellectual discussions, this is evident in the fact that we criticize one another about what we think, holding our adversaries directly or indirectly responsible for alleged misjudgments.[7] Whenever we consider normal human beings, we cannot avoid the fact of their volitional conduct, of actions they choose to bring about on their own—as self-responsible individuals.[8] When we introspect, when we look inward at our own consciousness, we realize that we have the capacity to choose among real alternatives and that we do so constantly.

It is a reasonable point of view, then, that human beings are first and foremost individuals who cause much of what they do. Their actions flow from their thinking, and their thinking is the sphere in which they are free, self-determined.[9] Individuals are unique and self-responsible.

CLASSICAL LIBERALISM, HUMAN NATURE, AND INDIVIDUALITY

Such considerations undermine the collectivist view that *human beings are primarily parts of a social whole.* Once we acknowledge clearly that individuals are thinking, acting "wholes" unto themselves, the metaphor of society as organism is exposed as just that—a metaphor. Society "as a whole" has no independent life—no ability to think, act, or value as an independent unit. All the thinking and acting, all the life-living, is done by the individuals comprising the society.

Given the falsity of the collectivist notion of human nature, it should come as no surprise that it is also impractical, tending when invoked to serve as a cover for the promotion of the special or vested privileges of some members of society (some *individuals*) at the expense of other members of society (other *individuals*).[10] The equating of special or vested interests with often vague, purportedly universal values or goals has indeed been a major source of political acrimony throughout human history, and it poisons contemporary democratic politics as well. If humans were primarily species-beings, at some point in the historical progress of collectivism we might expect human agents to succeed in shucking their illusory individual interests and acting in undivided unison with the rest of the human organism. But this hasn't even happened in communist nations, where competing interests have been ruthlessly suppressed or ignored.

As we observe various politically engaged individuals and interest groups jostling with each other and pursuing their special agendas in the name of the national or global good, it is easy to grow cynical. Such cynicism, however, is not an inevitable feature of political life. It is the result of trying to practice the impractical. A general acceptance of our rational, volitional, and individual natures as human beings would foster a more benevolent kind of social and political order, one in which each of us is recognized as sovereign and treated as sovereign. In such an order, our individual goals would be accepted as worthy and meaningful (at least potentially), and we could freely pursue them—but we could not impose them on anyone else. The interests that are truly common to all of us respect our nature as individuals and would certainly include the protection of property rights and other allied human rights—such as appropriate rights to associate with other individuals and groups.

It is classical liberalism that, more than any other political philosophy, acknowledges the individuality and worth of each person. There's always been a little bit of emphasis on individuality, of course, in various rebellious political movements, but it's very difficult to maintain the supremacy of the tribe or the state if one admits (and fully acts upon) the fact that what is truly important in a human society is the individuals who inhabit it as individuals. This is due to the fact that one can't reasonably say, "Well, we can do away with that individual or with that group of individuals or their projects so as to benefit some others, including some collective such as the state, community, culture, or race."

Indeed, with the recognition and acknowledgment of the supreme value of the individual, the very definition of a "good" or "just" society would have to emphasize the freedom and happiness of individuals, for society would be seen as consisting of nothing else but those distinct individuals. The "common good" looked to would be the common *individual* good: what each individual needs to flourish in cooperation with others in society. And the most important and fundamental need of that kind is freedom.

In fact, a characteristic of the classical liberal political ethos is that it enjoins scrutiny of a society on the basis of how loyal its governing institutions are to the mission of securing the rights of all individuals to their liberty and pursuit of happiness. In this respect it can be said that classical liberalism is actually a very prominent movement in the world today. It's not a pure or consistent movement, to be sure, but all those human rights organizations that go from country to country to check whether they adhere to tenets of justice are at least rhetorically committed to discovering whether the legal authorities treat human beings under their jurisdiction as individuals who have basic rights. Are the lives and projects of individual citizens being respected or treated with callous disregard?

FLUCTUATING CLASSES

The respect for individuality is one of the reasons that in a largely liberal—or let us say, to avoid confusion with American liberalism, a largely libertarian—society, membership in a class loses its moral and political significance. I once worked as a busboy in Cleveland, Ohio, and found that when I was paid, I could return to the same restaurant and eat a meal there. There was no frowning, head-shaking, or muttering, "Wait a minute, you don't belong here." In much of Europe, by contrast, if you work in a restaurant you don't get to eat there—although doing so is no longer illegal, it's certainly considered gauche.

In a more or less libertarian social-political society, the divisions that are based on incidental attributes—such as one's wealth, color, national origin, ethnicity, and race—tend to be less significant because one's individual worth trumps all these; classes, at any rate, are always in flux. Even racial and ethnic categories, not to mention religious or economic ones, tend to shift (through interracial marriage, religious conversion, and so forth), for there are no widespread and well-entrenched legal barriers to entry or exit.

Class categories and the behavior associated with them may still prevail in certain special contexts. For example, a professor will usually attain special respect in the classroom, but when one meets the professor at a restaurant, one need not carry over the behavior associated with that classroom status. No "Herr Doctor, Doctor" in the United States as still prevails, for example, in much of Germany.

The blurring or erasure of class boundaries can be a bit disturbing at times. It can sometimes encourage disrespect for people who in fact deserve respect. Rampant individualism can collapse into contempt for all authority. Such undiscriminating disrespect can be, but by no means need be, motivated by the idea that individuals matter primarily as individuals and not so much as members of classes. It is also, however, evident enough that we are social beings, members of the class of human beings, and that there are very important implications of that, too, which can be integrated into an individualist ethos. It would be unfair to suggest that individualism as such either implies or mandates social disintegration.

INDIVIDUALISM: TRUE AND FALSE

All the same, the association of individualism with classical liberalism has often been somewhat uncomfortable. The reason for this is that some have indeed overemphasized the element of individuality, seeming to imply that we are not also members of communities nor even of the human race. Such "atomistic" individualism has made it seem that classical liberalism is tied to a misguided social philosophy. An example of it may be found in the story of Robinson Crusoe, which is oft repeated by economists. If one models human life on Crusoe's story and his interaction with Friday, it appears that we are born capable of self-sufficient productive conduct and from the start choose whether to associate with others. Yet this idea is patently absurd, considering that all human beings are born helpless and grow up in the company of others on whose support they vitally depend.[11]

In any case, it is not true that individualism is necessarily committed to atomism. One can fully admit to the communal aspects of human life while insisting that we are essentially individuals as well. Such a robust individualism—what I have called "classical" individualism—also stresses the importance of the private realm and insists that all bona fide human communities must adhere to the terms individuals set for themselves.

The crucial individualist ingredient of classical liberal social and political theory stresses not some arid independence or isolation of the individual human being but the fact that everyone can in principle make independent judgments about the kind of communities that would be suitable to join. Given human nature, the element of choice must be preserved in every viable human community. This is the source of the classical liberal political principle that demands that the consent of the governed be upheld in public policy as well as in personal relations. In terms of this classical or moderate individualism, first found in the philosophy of Aristotle,[12] acts such as murder, assault, kidnapping, rape, robbery, and burglary are naturally enough understood as criminal ones, as coercive violations of justified rights.

INDIVIDUALITY AND PRIVACY

One implication of individualism, then, is that no one may be "used" by another without consent, because each individual is important and valuable in his or her own right. If an individual is important as such, then there is a sphere that constitutes the individual's realm of sovereignty and that others ought to respect: a realm within which one is free to make effective judgments about one's life. Indeed, in classical liberal, political, and legal theory there's a great deal of emphasis on individual rights rather than rights of families or other groups, and this derives from this individualist element of the position. The right to private property is, in turn, the most practically relevant of those individual rights.

The term *privacy* underscores this aspect of the importance of individuals. The right to *private* property is really just an extension, within the framework of a naturalist worldview, of the right to one's own life. It is when one engages with the rest of the world in one's unique (individual!) way that protection of the products of one's personal doings becomes important.[13] A respected right to private property will then make it possible to actualize and to protect one's identify and one's manifestation in the world—such as one's art, productivity, creativity, and innovation. Moreover, none of these may be used by others without the consent of the individual to whom they belong.

THE MORAL STANDING OF PRIVATE PROPERTY RIGHTS

So individualism underlies the regime of private property rights. Why, then, do we need a separate discussion of the merits of the right to private property? What will such an inquiry yield?

There are at least two answers to that question. First, when you resist people who are taking something from you by force, taxation, theft, or any other means, it is important to know even if only implicitly that the resistance is justified—that it is morally legitimate self-defense, akin to resisting someone who is assaulting or raping someone else. When someone robs another who resists, the latter has a commonsense idea of doing the right thing and knows that the resistance is not merely some immature, capricious, and willful conduct. It is not as if one were simply engaged in foot-stomping and crying, "I want it! I want it! I want it!" No; one senses that there is right on one's side, not just an arbitrary wish and desire. For moral and self-responsible beings, it is vital to know that one is in the right when one insists on the integrity of ownership—not merely being stubborn or antisocial, as opponents of a libertarian legal order often insist. Without that conviction, one's resistance might be half-hearted or even become completely deflated.

Second, the social regulative principle of a right to private property is the most important, practical, public policy element of the individualist and classical liberal worldview. An individualist would argue that when private property is not respected and not sufficiently protected within a community, something is wrong with that community—it is not quite fit for human inhabitation, given the individuality of every person and the necessity of respect for this individuality as a precondition for his or her flourishing. If individualism is indeed sound, so is the principle of private property rights; therefore, a specific defense of property rights should reinforce and clarify the overall framework of individualism.

BEYOND PRODUCTIVITY

There are many different ways that private property has been argued for in the history of political economy. Most prominent has been the claim that there should be legal protection of the right to private property because this facilitates productivity—a point in agreement with Marx but universalized beyond a given epoch. Protecting this right helps society get rich—not only in the sixteenth century, but always. Both Adam Smith and John Stuart Mill tended to argue along these lines, and many economists today argue a similar point. Indeed, that is one reason why many governments are now engaging in privatization: to encourage economic growth.

All of this is important but not what is *most* important. From an individualist perspective, each individual has these rights regardless of what's done when she is simply exercising them. Each individual is an end in herself. It is individuals that are the important element of society, not some outsider, not some entity such as society, the community, the tribe, or the ethnic group. Even if particular individuals waste away their lives, they have that right, for that life is theirs to waste away. Each individual's life belongs to herself, and to live it requires the exercise of her own choice and self-responsibility. But choice implies alternatives. The freedom required to live a life well—living honorably, fulfilling one's potential, and achieving excellence—thus *entails* the freedom to live it badly.

It is this aspect of liberty, the right to choose how one lives, that is most central to human community life, even if (indeed, because) for the sake of one's personal life it is equally important to make the right choice, to choose to do the right thing.

This is why the right to private property is vital. When respected and effectively protected, it secures for human individuals a sphere of personal jurisdiction, the right to acquire and hold the props with which to order one's life. Moral virtues such as generosity, kindness, courage, moderation, and prudence are all imperatives, the practice of which engages one with the natural world. If one is not in charge of some of that world, or at least in charge of oneself, one cannot conduct oneself virtuously. So the rights to one's life, liberty, and property are necessary conditions for a morally significant or meaningful life in human communities.

NO CARTE BLANCHE TO COMMUNITIES

It needs to be stressed here that even if we are essentially individuals, this doesn't mean that we are not also naturally members of societies. As moral agents and as candidates for membership in some human communities or societies, however, it is our moral responsibility to judge those societies on the basis of whether they do adequate justice to our individuality. If we are free to flourish as individuals, we will flourish as a society.

It follows that we must always keep in mind the question of whether we ought to live in a given community. Do we want to—ought we to—support this particular kind of public policy, this kind of a legal system? What is the standard by which we make such a decision when we have the chance? At the most basic level of community concern must lie the issue of what principles should govern human communities. The right to private property is one of those principles.

Very often we don't have the ability to act on the choices we make about basic principles, but at least we can think about them so that when we do get a chance to make a significant decision, we will know where we stand. We owe it to ourselves, to a life of integrity, not to forget about that issue, ever. That is the highest duty of citizenship!

PROPERTY RIGHTS, INDIVIDUALITY, AND THE MORAL LIFE

As we have seen, if we as individuals are to lead our lives by our judgments, it is crucial that we control the elements with which our lives are lived. The right to private property secures a sphere in which we can act. The question, How ought I to live? becomes the foremost question to which you then seek an answer.

Few people ever quite let go of the idea that some things that people do are good and some are bad; that those who perform the actions are the ones responsible for the goodness or badness of the deeds. When we reflect upon our lives, we say, "I did or didn't do the right thing." Moreover, we can go on to consider what we did with what belongs to us—whether we used it well or badly. Although most of us aren't moral philosophers by profession, that question, How ought I to live? is still always near the forefront of our minds. No matter what you do, even reading these lines, the question will arise of what you *should* do: Should I sleep or should I pay attention? Should I consider this point or just glide over it?

All such questions pertain to one's ethical agency, one's governance of one's life, one's sovereignty. The conviction that one is doing the right thing becomes crucial if one is indeed the master of one's existence.

Now, without the right to private property, without those "props," without some elements of reality that are under our jurisdiction, our ethical decisions cannot be effectual.

Consider, for example, the situation if it turns out to be true that a good human being ought to be generous. Well, if we do not have the right to private property, how are we going to be generous? Are we going to emulate politicians and bureaucrats and simply expropriate what belongs to others and give this to the poor and needy? That's not generosity. That's theft. Without a definite sphere of sovereignty that is manifest in the actual world where we live our lives, we would not be able to act on most moral principles, especially those that involve the disposition of resources. Are we stingy? But one has to be stingy *with something.* If one is a neat person, one has to be neat within some sphere that one keeps orderly. If one is a slob, one will need something that isn't receiving good care. If those items don't belong to you, if you always have to ask permission of society, clan, tribe, or nation to do something with these things, then you are not the effective agent in the disposition of them, and you are then not an effective moral agent either. You cannot take pride in what you achieve or feel guilt for your failings. You are basically just a cell in a larger organism, a cog in a wheel. You are still a human being with free will, but the kinds of alternatives you now face become very constricted—mainly, whether to obey or disobey.

In short, then, in order to lead an effective life of moral virtue, we must have the right to property, be free to acquire, hold, and then to part with specific material values on our own terms.

THE VIRTUE OF PRUDENCE

Prudence is one of the virtues identified in classical Greece. I want now to discuss it in some detail.

In the modern era, prudence has been demeaned. Ever since the era of Thomas Hobbes, the task of taking care of oneself and one's own has been deemed to be instinctual. Hobbes argued that we are all *driven* to preserve ourselves, but he made his case by extrapolating the principles of classical mechanistic physics to human life, a move that is not at all justified. In fact, human beings must choose their conduct, including whether they will serve their own well-being or that of others. Prudence, as the ancients saw it, is the virtue one needs to take decent care of oneself.

Later, Immanuel Kant argued that since prudence is a motivation that is aligned to one's own interest or inclinations, it is not a moral virtue. According to Kant, only motives that are totally indifferent to one's own interest or inclinations can have moral significance, even though we cannot know whether we are ever so purely motivated.

Neither Hobbes nor Kant had it right. Prudence is a moral virtue, though not the only or highest one. In any case, a prudent person acts, among other ways, economically. Such a person realizes that one must reserve for the future by putting resources away for a rainy day. Such a person isn't reckless in the disposition of the resources over which he or she has control.

If we have no right to acquire or hold things, then we can't be prudent because we don't have the decision-making authority to govern resources in accordance with standards of prudence. On the other hand, if we do have this authority, then we can choose to act prudently.

PRUDENCE AND JUSTICE

If in fact it is a moral virtue to be prudent, but it is politically impossible to act on that virtue, then there is a basic conflict be-

tween ethics and politics. Then the political sphere is not properly *adjusted* to the ethical sphere. Then our ethical agency has
not been done sufficient justice by the legal system in which we
act.

Indeed, that is one of the things that are so frustrating in societies in which one lacks the right to private property. Not
only is one thwarted in efforts to acquire life's necessities, but
one cannot even act responsibly at all. Here what happens is a
version of the tragedy of the commons.

The tragedy of the commons is usually associated with
management of the environment. The reason for this is that
most spheres that suffer persistent environmental problems are
public ones. The atmosphere, oceans, rivers, large forests, and so
on are realms in which no one is individually responsible. To
put it another way, everyone is responsible for the management
of such spheres but no one has a clear idea what to do about
this responsibility without the constraints imposed by private
property rights.

When you have a distinct or definite sphere of jurisdiction,
however complicated it may be—with various layers of responsibility and delegation—then when something is done wrong,
responsibility can be traced to the agent or agents who did it.
When something is done right, again responsibility can be
traced to the agent or agents whose job it was to do them right.
Without the right to private property, this sort of accountabil-
ity is impossible.

This is one reason why no society can completely abolish
private property: It is impossible to act in any sort of responsible way without *some* sphere of personal jurisdiction.

MORAL STANDING OF
POLITICAL-ECONOMIC SYSTEMS

When the Left morally criticizes classical liberals because the
liberal or libertarian polity makes profit-making possible, what
is the answer? It's not enough to just say, "Well, we just like to

make profit." A murderer can say, "I just like to kill people." Clearly, the mere stipulation of a preference is no justification.

One of the questions that arise in the discussion of political philosophy and political economy is whether these disciplines have moral standing. There are those who argue that a social science such as economics requires nothing from morality—indeed, that it is entirely amoral, purely positive or descriptive in its central thrust. But this is a mistake. All human affairs, including economic ones, are permeated with moral issues. In economics, for example, there is the moral (or, as Rasmussen and Den Uyl have called it, the meta-normative) element of private property rights.[14]

Private property rights sustain trade and commerce. In order to trade goods and services—in order to sell, produce, save, or hoard them—you have to have some level of jurisdiction over them. If I am to trade my watch for your shirt, then it has to be *my* watch or I must be the delegated authority of the watch's owner, and it has to be *your* shirt. Otherwise, we would have no ability or justification to engage in this trade. I can't sell you something that belongs to another. Moreover, if it belongs to everyone all at once, no one can sell or trade it and chaos prevails with regard to its use. So commerce, as well as charity and generosity, presupposes the institution of private property rights. Without that institution, these activities cannot be undertaken smoothly, without confusion.

If one does not own anything, no trade can ensue and all the talk of supply and demand must be abandoned in favor of what collectivists tend to support, a sort of share-and-share-alike "economy." But to own something means to be in a distinctively normative relationship with others. They are prohibited from taking what belongs to someone else. They ought not do so and will be penalized, furthermore, if they do.

So the amoral stance on the market economy is doomed to failure. What is needed is a moral justification of the institution of private property rights.[15] To accomplish this, we must analyze human nature as it is manifested in the natural world. Will such an analysis support the institutions of freedom and free markets and give them a stronger moral standing in human society than alternative ones possess?

MORALITY AND PUBLIC AFFAIRS

Now there are some who would spurn the prospect of a fully free society because of the possibility in such a society that innocent and helpless persons will meet with natural disaster and find themselves without any voluntary help when they need it. That is certainly a possibility, even if not a likelihood, in a free society. James Sterba, for example, has been arguing for decades that because such cases are possible, the victims involved have a right to welfare that the legal order may protect. Such positive rights, whereby people are required to work for other persons—or part with goods they have worked for in order to support others—come about because it would not be reasonable, Sterba argues, to demand that such people respect private property rights. It would be more reasonable to expect of them to strive to obtain the goods they need—ones Sterba calls, in a question-begging fashion, surplus wealth. (As if someone could be justified in identifying what constitutes "surplus"—a term from classical Marxism that makes no sense outside of the Marxist framework.)

If one recognizes, however, that an individual's life is his own and that he does not belong to anything or anyone outside of memberships to which he or she consents, then even the most dire needs of others cannot justify any institutional arrangement that fails to recognize individual rights—to life, liberty, and, yes, property. Just as it is unjustified to use others as a shield against natural danger, one may not use others, nor the wealth they own, in any respect against their will. One must find ways around this prohibition, as indeed most do when they engage in trade rather than theft in the effort to acquire their own wealth.

It is reasonable to demand this of everyone, even those in dire straits. If, however, in desperate circumstances, such people do not honor this prohibition, there can be some measure of forgiveness, even within the purview of the legal authority (as per some cases that have been subject to unusual judicial discretion). But hard cases make bad law. Even victims of circumstance benefit greatly from life in a polity that respects and protects the rights of each individual person. Indeed, it can be argued that the victims and the disasters multiply when such rights are not on principle respected.

THE PURSUIT OF WEALTH VERSUS THE IDEA OF THE DIVIDED SELF

So the right to private property is the concrete manifestation of the possibility of responsible conduct in a community in which people need to know what they ought to do and with what they ought to do it, and moreover, that respect and protection of private property rights make possible the pursuit of wealth.

Oddly, however, that fostering of wealth production is a *criticism* many offer against the system of free market capitalism that is built on the legal infrastructure of private property rights. Along with Marx, they argue that private property rights—if they are protected, maintained, and developed as law—encourage a hedonistic, narrowly selfish life, one that is concerned exclusively with acquiring worldly goods. As Marx said in his famous essay, "On the Jewish Question," "The right of man to property is the . . . right of selfishness." Freedom is supposed to make too much self-indulgence, including pleasure, possible.

So another question arises: Is pleasure justified? For even if the right to private property could be used for purposes quite different from obtaining pleasure in life, if pleasure is something loathsome and this right somehow encourages its relentless pursuit, perhaps it is an institution that does more harm than good.

We cannot enter this topic at length, but we can note that if we are indeed natural beings in this world, one of our important values will be pleasure, the good feelings we experience via our bodies. This is so even if there are higher goods, the attainment of which may require giving up some pleasure. If pleasure can be a value, and if wealth brings with it the possibility of pleasure, then wealth itself is a worthy good—provided that it is not stolen but created or produced, and that it is not chosen as the highest good if a higher one can be identified.

Now, clearly, we are talking about a life lived within the context of the natural world. But if one has a completely different point of view of human nature, whereby only the spiritual side of human life is of significance, then one will embrace a different system of values and probably also champion different institutions. We have a powerful tradition in most civilizations whereby there is an uneasiness about facilitating the flourishing of the human body. That is often what stands, at a most basic level, against the free society!

Many elements of classical liberalism or libertarianism, including the right to private property, assume that we have a task to live properly in the midst of a natural environment, a natural world. We are not just living a purely immaterial life. Food needs to be grown and distributed, production has to occur. All sorts of concrete, natural tasks need to be carried out in order to facilitate our human lives.

If our bodies are nonexistent and the material world in which we live is only an illusion, then such temporal matters are of no account. If this natural life turns out to be either illusory or insignificant, politics might indeed be subject to different principles, principles that facilitate goals different from prosperity, flourishing, and other kinds of earthly success. It's not easy to imagine what those goals would be. Yet, in a philosophical discussion of these issues, one has to contend with the fact that alternative ideas about the basic elements of human living are indeed proposed. Liberalism has to stand the test of being compared with these alternative pictures.

There are doctrines in the world that say that all individuality, for example, is a myth. In addition to the Marxists and other collectivist views we have discussed, there are Eastern religions that contend that the natural, individual self is an illusion and that, in truth, we're all just part of the universal consciousness.

In order to test this, however, one has to have some criteria by which truth can be determined. The naturalist approach rests on the application of criteria that are universally accessible, that is, available to all human beings with their rational faculties intact. The alternatives tend to be very vaguely and confusedly supported. Their appeal tends to be more psychological than logical, their conclusions more asserted than proved.

One source of the popularity of such views is the lack of a clear, unambiguous, and benign acceptance of our earthly selves. We often think ourselves to be so unique, so extraordinary that we believe we must be partly divine or otherworldly. St. Augustine said it well when he cried,

> How great, my God, is this force of memory, how exceedingly great! It is like a vast and boundless subterranean shrine. . . . Yet this is a faculty of my mind and belongs to my nature; nor can I myself grasp all that I am. Therefore the mind is not large enough to contain itself. But where can that uncontained part of it be?[16]

He then answered, as have millions of others, that it must be somewhere apart from nature.

Hence the moral taint imputed to business and the marketplace. If our natural selves are somehow inferior, then servicing them with vigor, as successful businesspeople do, must be misguided. People who pursue profit or material wealth would then be pursuing trivia. They would be mere hedonists. Such doctrines are hard to live by consistently, and in modern industrial civilization we often pay them little more than lip service—we praise Mother Teresa and then hit the shopping malls. We live a schizophrenic life. We embrace the values of prosperity, economic success, and wealth on the one hand, but deny it on the other.

Yet, if in our practical daily lives we embrace our bodies, minds, emotions, sensations, and so on, then we suggest by this that a more integrated view of how to live and how to protect our values is appropriate—not one that tears us into warring pieces.

A PLATONIC HERITAGE

The idea of the divided self started with Plato, at least with a certain reading of him. Plato regards our minds as divided from our bodies and argues that the mind must hold the rest of our self in check and rule it firmly. The human self, by this view, consists of essentially disparate and warring factions. Major writers, especially theologians, have stressed this drama ever since, and it is reflected in our society's institutions. Victor Hugo noted its Christian incarnation:

> On the day when Christianity said to man: You are a dual-ity, you are composed of two beings, one perishable, the other immortal, one carnal, the other ethereal, one en-chained by appetites, needs, and passions, the other lofted on wings of enthusiasm and reverie, the former bending for-ever to earth, its mother, the latter soaring always toward heaven, its fatherland—on that day, the drama was created. Is it anything other, in fact, than this contrast on every day, this battle at every moment, between two opposing princi-ples that are ever-present in life and that contend over man from the cradle to the grave?[17]

Even secular thinkers like Adam Smith implicitly accept this dichotomization into two sides of the human self when he notes, in a famous remark, "It is not from the benevolence of the butcher, the brewer, or the baker, that we expect our din-ner, but from their regard for their own interest. We address ourselves, not to their humanity but to their self-love, and never talk to them of our own necessities but of their advantages."[18] Why *juxtapose* our humanity with our advantage? Aristotle and other ancients didn't when they accepted prudence as a bona fide moral virtue—as an *expression* of our humanity.

As a result of this popularization of our allegedly divided self, many of us are often apologetic when pursuing a satisfactory, happy life here on planet Earth. Then we find it difficult if not impossible to defend the political regime that most clearly enhances such a life, becoming defensive when others maintain that it is only a mundane, materialist life that such a regime supports. The notion of the divided self is probably responsible, more than anything else, for the unrelenting moral disdain exhibited in most cultures toward capitalism, even while as a practical matter the system simply cannot be dispensed with.

Mind you, there are many people with a dualistic bent—for example, Acton, Cobden, Bright, Bastiat, and Tocqueville—who have favored the liberal political order. That is not at issue here. They are not able to show the morally compelling merits of capitalism insofar as they are bound by the view that the pursuits of this world are not so vital to human beings as are the pursuits of a supernatural one. Prudence implies concern for economic prosperity as a legitimate priority only if the self whose well-being is to be looked after is the living, actual self of this world. If it is not, if the vital elements of the human self pertain to one's afterlife, then the moral imperative to seek to prosper in life can easily be undercut by the moral imperative to prepare for the afterlife. This preparation may indeed require forgoing the prosperity that is possible in this one.

By contrast, the regime of private property rights rests, in part, on an integrated understanding of human life. It rejects the common idea that each human being is fundamentally divided. It places us squarely on the earth, even though it is by no means hostile to anyone who chooses to look elsewhere for fulfillment—quite the contrary. Indeed, the right to private property has made religious pursuits extremely fruitful as well as abundant, especially in the United States, where churches can purchase their own land and welcome parishioners undisrupted by their foes.

The fact that dualism undermines the case for a free, capitalist, classical liberal order does not mean that no dualists have supported one, only that this support has been vulnerable to criticism from within their own frame of reference. That alone is reason why the idea of the divided human self must be seriously rethought. Without serious modification of it, based on the evidence of everyday lives and history, the best socioeconomic system human beings have ever identified will fail to gain moral standing and to flourish.

CONCLUSION

What has been said here is by no means a thorough defense of the right to private property, but it does furnish some hints as to how such a defense would have to be presented when the issue arises, which is quite often in our world. First, this right, if protected, preserves one's moral agency in this natural world in which community life occurs. Furthermore, it underscores the fact that striving to prosper is a morally valid goal for human beings. The moral virtue of prudence, of taking the requisite actions to care for oneself and one's intimates, supports the right to private property as well.

9

THE DEMOCRATIC IDEAL

Democracy is a process by which some decisions are made. In the context of politics, it means the kind of system that depends upon the participation of the citizenry for certain purposes and that gives majorities the ultimate power to decide what should happen. What grounds democracy as a just mode of political decision making is that citizens have the ultimate authority concerning certain matters in the polis. The reason they do have this ultimate authority is that they are, as adults, equal in their status vis-à-vis the stake they have in their political institutions, their laws, public policies, foreign relations, and the like. That they have this equal status hinges on certain extra or prepolitical matters, to be discerned by way of reflection upon human nature and proper human relations. For now, I'll simply note that as I understand political matters, they arise from the moral fact that each individual adult human being has as his or her task in life to live it rationally, to flourish as a rational animal. Since this task for adults can only be achieved if they are not subject to another's will—in which case another's rational choice would be the ruling principle of their lives—in communities human beings must be sovereign. From this it follows that they must have a say in their own political fate, ergo, democracy.

In any case, democracy is derivative of what human beings are taken to be as they find themselves within a community that aims at justice, a polity. From the Hobbesian framework, democracy is recommended because all of us are nothing but bits of matter in motion and thus lack any significant, fundamental differentiating attributes. Even our human nature is but nominal, a status in the world established by means of the human intellect's response to the motions that affect the brain, a response itself motivated by the drive for self-preservation or keeping in continued motion in part by naming groups of impulses effecting the brain. We make the categories, creating them by naming our sensory input as we will.[1] So the reason for democracy à la the Hobbesian view is that nothing justifies differentiating some people from others; indeed, if one were to be fully consistent, nothing justifies differentiating anything from anything else, at the metaphysical, fundamental level of being. A somewhat different reason for democracy arises from the Lockean view, one closer to what I sketched above as my own. For Locke, at least when we turn to his political treatise, we are all equal and independent in the state of nature, that is, prior to the formation of or apart from civil society or the polis. Adult human beings begin, regardless of the precise point at which each of them reaches adulthood, as equally embarking on a human life, one that is to be governed by the laws of nature, which is reason if one but consult it. In other words, we are all moral agents having to live up to our moral responsibilities or duties, and in this we are all alike. So we are all endowed with natural rights, which spell out for each of us a sphere of sovereignty, also known as personal authority or jurisdiction. There are no natural masters or natural slaves, although there may be borderline cases of defective or crucially incapacitated persons. If this is kept in clear focus, one will realize that a human community starts with no one superior or inferior regarding the issue of the authority to make law and to govern. Thus, democracy.

But democracy is a process that is morally required by the right to take part in deciding or to give consent. It is in fact our natural right to person and estate that lies behind the right to be part of the decision-making process involved in politics. It is not a process that is applicable to everything one might want to influence, however. There is a proper sphere of democracy.

Clearly there are those who propose that democracy is un-limited—only the fact that people will things to be one way or another matters. Some interpreters of Locke—for example, Wilmore Kendall and his followers—have claimed this, as have some conservatives (e.g., Robert Bork).[2] Thus they argue that once human beings are no longer in a state of nature, they have in effect adopted democracy as a decision-making process re-garding whatever comes up for public discussion and whatever a sizable number of them want to subject to this process.

Yet this seems to me to be wrong, whatever the proper in-terpretation of Locke might be, and I would dispute that Locke can be coherently interpreted this way. In Locke, the justifica-tion for government lies in the need for the protection of nat-ural rights, a protection not easily obtained (except by the strong) in the state of nature. Moreover, the state of nature need not be a source of much intellectual consternation—it refers to any circumstance not governed by due process or the rule of law, one we may even encounter in a back alley or away from civilization where we can be easy prey for thugs. In the classic movie, *The Man Who Shot Liberty Valance,* it was the situation prior to when John Wayne enabled Jimmy Stuart to establish law and order. In actual life, it is the situation one may face in the middle of the Mojave Desert or in any inner-city park where law enforcement is nearly nil.

So Locke sees the protection of everyone's natural rights as the proper purpose of government. Since establishing, main-taining, and protecting government is itself a form of human ac-tivity that can be done well or badly, it must be guided by the principles of natural rights—its creation, development, and op-erations may not encroach upon those rights, lest its proper pur-pose be undermined. Perhaps the best way to understand this is by recalling the commonsense notion that even the securing of highly valued goals does not justify the employment of immoral means.

Quite apart from Locke, in any case, unless democracy is itself guided by norms—unless the people express and implement their will as they should and not as they should not—it becomes self-defeating. Not only is there the problem that such a process is in violation of the rights of innocents who would be made victims of the use of arbitrary force. Unlimited democracy, furthermore, can undo democracy itself. If democracy, for example, is applied too broadly, it is bent upon defeating its very purpose: the goal that justifies its employment. To provide a hint via a possible result of the democratic process, suppose that we democratically vote to exclude some people from the voting process. This is a legacy of some state governments in the United States, as well as the efforts of the federal government. When the possibility of voting is linked to property ownership or some other condition, the democratic process is weakened. It also occurs when the federal government focuses on what has come to be called inclusiveness so that, for the sake of including in the governing process members of some minority groups, it is decided that other members should be given lower representation. Such group inclusiveness undermines the natural rights of individuals to take part in the political process, a right that derives from their right to liberty of association. Yet the underlying justification for democracy is that individuals have the right to consent to their government. In other words, if the democratic process can justifiably produce governmental measures that violate the natural rights of individuals, this undermines the capacity of these individuals to be full, equally free participants in the democratic process.

Other kinds of cases abound. If by the democratic process the rights to life, liberty, or property could justifiably be abrogated or violated, those taking part in the process no longer can act freely and independently. The majority can threaten their free judgments and can enact measures that will authorize vindictive official actions against the minority, something that inevitably leads to the undermining of democracy. That is just why the "democracies" of Eastern Europe were a complete farce despite the great numbers of participants in the actual electoral process. Its parties had no liberty to vote as they wanted, for whom they wanted.

Arguably, of course, democracy is needed to get any kind of legal system going, even an anarchist one, since before decent laws can be instituted or established, they require serious support. If that support is given by a solid enough majority, it (1) can resist rejecting by many who might hesitate but see benefit in the association, and (2) may set into motion a lasting and stable noncoercive legal order. Even in such a legal order, however, there will have to be decisions made that are not unanimous, akin to the way in which a civil court jury decides not by unanimous but by majority vote.

Once the system of laws is in place, if, when I vote, I know that voting my conscience will result in having my sovereignty undermined, leading to my partial enslavement or involuntary servitude, I will not likely vote my conscience. I will act like the victim of the mugger who is told, "Your money or your life!" When I hand over my money, I do it under compulsion and not by choice. It is a myth that we always have a choice, for a choice that is set out by others regarding one's life, that robs one of one's life and takes away the prospects of a self-governed future, is no choice. If a democratic process allows a similar act on the part of the majority, the members of the minority will vote— voice their judgment and indicate their preferences—under severe constraint. No true will of the majority can emerge under these circumstances.

We can extend this analysis now to the realm of contemporary politics in Western democracies. Let's focus on the general situation in the United States today.

Whenever public programs are being cut, those who have their benefits reduced offer cries of need and those who feel for them cries of compassion. Yet whenever public programs are proposed that also cut out the benefits of those who need to pay for it from higher taxes, it is contended that this is just the result of social life. After all, "we" have decided to fund social security, unemployment compensation, the national parks, and public broadcasting, haven't we? So it is no objection to this that some of us suffer losses, now have to forgo benefits, and experience reduced income that can lead to reduced quality of education, recreation, home life, dental care, transportation safety, cultural enrichment, and so forth. None of this is supposed to matter because "we" have decided to tax ourselves higher to fund all those public programs. Why is it okay to violate the individual rights to liberty and property of millions of people when the majority of us decide to do this but not okay to reduce the benefits of people when a somewhat differently configured majority of us decided to do that? Why may the choices of some individuals be ignored and thwarted by democratic decision making but not those of others trumped by the same process? The fact is that most people who talk of and like democracy in the context of the currently bloated understanding do so only when it supports their agenda. It is fine to use democracy to rob the rich—it makes it valid public policy instead of theft—but if the poor are the targets, then suddenly democracy is invalid.

Indeed, the reason for this is, as suggested earlier, that democracy is never enough. There must always be some specification of the goals for which democracy is appropriate. It isn't enough to have a democratic process—it can lead to results of widely different quality. Sometimes the majority does right, sometimes wrong. The task of political theory is, in part, to identify those areas of public life that should be subject to democratic decision making.

What are those areas? And why are they the ones?

Whether alone or with his or her fellows, a human being may not do some things to other human beings. In particular, no one may take over another's life. This is so whether that other's life is fortunate, well to do, talented, accomplished, beautiful, accepted by others, and freely granted benefits. In short, neither the fortunate and accomplished, nor those lacking in good fortune, are available for others to be used when permission hasn't been granted, when consent is not given. In either kind of case, no one person or group may take over another's life—it amounts to the kind of crime that may be classified as theft, robbery, assault, kidnapping, murder, battery, and rape. The fact that the numbers of those who do such things is increased and even constitute a majority of those concerned makes no difference. Nor does the fact that some procedure has been followed as these policies are instituted, for lacking the explicit or at least tacit consent of those who are to be deprived makes any such process invalid, unjust, and undue.

It is wrong to steal on one's own as well as with the support of millions. It is wrong to enslave others, to place others into servitude when they refuse, and the like, no matter whether one is in the minority or the majority. Nor can majorities authorize certain people, such as their political representatives, to carry out such deeds, even if they do it indirectly by threatening those whom they would rob, steal from, kidnap, assault, or whatever with aggressive enforcement at the hands of the police. It is wrong, then, even for the government of a representative democracy or republic to carry out such deeds. Having done it with democratic "authorization" makes it no more right than if no such authorization had taken place. There is simply no moral authority for anyone to delegate to another such powers since one hasn't got them in the first place. If my friends and I enact an elaborate process, surrounded with pomp and circumstance, ritual and ornamentation, to commence kidnapping your children or confiscating your wealth, all this is morally and politically trumped by the fact that your consent to the process has been lacking. Unless you are a criminal, who has by his or her crime in effect tacitly agreed to accept our forcible self-protective response, you may not be intruded upon.[3] Most of this is admitted by all the parties to the debate. This is why even when the people elect certain political representatives (for example, conservative Republicans), others (for example, liberal Democrats) often claim that what results, in terms of legislation, is wrong and should not have been done. They maintain this in various political forums that are supposedly the spheres of democratic decision making. So they evidently think that what the democratic process produces is not decisive as to what ought to be done. Even if a law passes, critics will call it wrong—heartless, unkind, lacking in compassion. Even supporters of legal positivism, who discount any moral dimension of the legislative process, such as the obligation to be guided by natural or divine law, will protest democratic attacks upon values other than democracy.[4] This is because no one simply accepts the answer to a challenge of a democratically arrived-at result that they find morally abhorrent: that, well, the result was brought about by way of the democratic process. "We" did it, so it's okay, a matter of society's collective will. Even in criminal trials, the mini-democracy of a jury verdict is governed by firm provisions of due process and with opportunities of appeal.

It is, then, no valid answer to those who protest the taking of their life—time, income, good fortune, or whatever—by majority vote, "Well, this is okay since it is done democratically." The violation of the rights of individuals is no less justified by democracy than is collective callousness. This raises the problem of how to be kind, compassionate, generous, and helpful to those in genuine need without violating the rights of individuals to their life, liberty, and property. The answer is actually quite simple: Do it, promote it, and exhibit it by your own conduct! When members of a society learn that moral principles cannot justly be violated by the democratic process, so they may not violate anyone's rights with the excuse that "we" did it so it's okay, they learn also that when the right thing must be done, it has to be done by choice, free of coercion.[5] The help that the poor and needy should be given must be given at the initiative of the free citizen—via charity, church, philanthropy, fund raising, and the like.

I would like to conclude by recalling the late Robert Nozick's reason for abandoning, at least for a while, his championing of the fully free society and by addressing his concerns, which are expressed, I think, quite eloquently and sincerely. I believe his sentiments echo those of many who would not wish to go all the way with the imperative to freedom.

> The libertarian position I once propounded now seems to me seriously inadequate, in part because it did not fully knit the human considerations and joint cooperative activities it left room for more closely into its fabric. It neglected the symbolic importance of an official political concern with issues or problems, as a way of marking their importance or urgency and hence of expressing, intensifying, channeling, encouraging, and validating our private actions and concerns toward them. Joint goals that the government ignores completely—it is different with private or family goals—tend to appear unworthy of our joint attention and hence to receive little. . . .[6]

This is a sad mistake. Nozick seems to lack the confidence that free men and women would forge a culture that gives clear enough expression to all human virtues, including generosity and benevolence in the shape of wide-scale philanthropy and provisions for emergency through charity and insurance in the name of which the coercive powers of the welfare state are established and defended. Yet if he were right to doubt the predominant goodness of free men and women, it is perplexing, to say the least, why he has hope for the same from government, that is, armed bureaucrats. First, the evidence is overwhelming that bureaucrats are ill-chosen as champions of any of the virtues other than certain narrow ones, such as fairness and punctuality, that are required from them at their administrative jobs. The growth of the welfare state has been accompanied at every step with scandals at every level of governance. The moral tragedy of the commons has manifested itself more and more with the enlargement of the commons. That is, fewer and fewer people see themselves as individually responsible for what occurs in our society, which leads to widespread demoralization at every level of human community life. Second, when governments take over the task of addressing major problems in health care, unemployment, catastrophic aid, and the like, the job is usually done willy-nilly, since bureaucrats are generally reluctant to work at these tasks with the determination that a professional, well-paid body of men and women would. The bureaucrat has to sustain his or her interest as a feeling of duty that, sadly, wanes rather rapidly once the job becomes routine. One need but recall the expression on the faces of most bureaucrats when one turns to them for support—say, at the postal, urban development, and social security offices. In the main, bureaucrats tend to find it a bother to come to the assistance of people naturally enough, since there is very little in it for them, even in the sense of satisfying some urge toward noble service. Rather, they tend to see their work as mostly a chore they aren't well enough paid to perform, the efficient, enthusiastic performance of which brings them little reward. There are, of course, some exceptions, but hardly enough to fulfill the sort of expectations on which the welfare state is founded.

Nozick's modulated Platonic hopes, to the effect that some guardian class will bring forth the best of the community, is difficult to explain other than, perhaps, by reference to the age-old propensity of philosophers to believe about themselves and those whom they befriend that they have a better handle on human virtues than do others and if only those who feel as they do were in charge, matters would be significantly improved. It's a myth. We are all equally capable of good and evil and thus the free society in which no power is monopolized by any class is more likely to bear just fruit than one where some elite assumes even moderate measures of control over the rest.

In one of his works, on classical liberalism, Ludwig von Mises hailed the free system for lacking any pomp, or all the trappings of passion and feeling, leaving it with no more than the endorsement of science or dispassionate reason. Actually, however, he was only half-right.

The free society is indeed recommended by reason, but not at the expense of the recognition of as well as enthusiasm for its supreme value. As Henry Hazlitt, another champion of liberty, put it: "The superior freedom of the capitalist system, its superior justice, and its superior productivity are not three superiorities, but one. The justice follows from the freedom and the productivity follows from the freedom and the justice."[7]

10

REVISITING CLASS WARFARE

When Karl Marx popularized the notion of class warfare—the view, advanced by many political economists in the heyday of classical economics, that in capitalism the rich and poor are always in combat with each other—there was something to his thesis. When capitalism started to emerge in Western culture, it followed centuries of feudalism and mercantilism, systems that explicitly accepted the idea of the class structure and ran the economy from the top down. People in that era used to fit into different strata of society, and their children and grandchildren were all stuck there with no hope of escape. There is still much evidence of this kind of social-economic life throughout the world, even in Western Europe, when one leaves the big cosmopolitan cities where the bourgeois live.

At the onset of near-capitalism, which had its greatest impetus in the birth of classical liberal ideas—individual liberty, property rights, the rule of law, political equality, and democracy—millions of people moved from rural regions of various societies into urban centers, seeking jobs that did not bind them and their families permanently to some lord and master. They didn't suddenly become wealthy! Rather, for the first time in human history, these people had some kind of chance to work their way up from utter poverty to economic opportunity and prosperity.

When Marx looked at the evidence, he still saw millions of workers on one side with a great many old and new rich people on the other. There hadn't been time to come even near to evening things out, as free markets tend to do—as in a marathon race, with a few up front, increasingly more following, the bulk in the middle, and the stragglers at the end, but with nearly all of it changing constantly. That sort of bell curve distribution developed with the increasing influence of free market institutions, and that is exactly what more recent supporters of capitalism expected, while its critics kept fixated on the past, the transition period, remaining skeptical about the prospects of the workers.

This pessimistic view tends to become a self-fulfilling prophecy. When you fear failure unreasonably, you urge upon political representatives the very measures that ensure it. If you keep insisting that the free market system encourages a society divided into the few haves and the many have-nots, politicians begin to make laws—high taxes, government regulation, and laws obstructing the free flow of commerce—regimenting market behavior, which is exactly what keeps the market from mixing it up good and hard so that all participants get a shot at success over and over again.

We are continuing to witness the works of prophets of doom. Some political analysts and many politicians repeat the myth about the widening gap between the rich and the poor. They are singing the favorite tune of leftist critics of the capitalist system.

Their most recent evidence of class warfare is that wages in the marketplace have tended to rise slowly, whereas on Wall Street the big, rich, powerful corporations are making huge profits. Ergo, the poor keep being poor, while the rich keep getting richer.

Look again. Wages are not where the action is, even for most hourly wage earners. Most of us who work for salaries or wages have all kinds of investments, from insurance to savings to pensions, which benefit from the strength of the stock market. The big corporations are big precisely because millions of working men and women own their stocks and have made it possible for them to produce the wide array of goods and services that the public likes and buys.

The big corporations are not owned by fat cats—although there will always be some entrepreneurs with talent who will make a bundle from how they are managed, as well as a few who rake in their inherited wealth. But those numbers are entirely negligible. There is no class warfare in capitalism. There is only the ongoing economic strivings of millions leading them to constantly changing places along the economic marathon race.

Also, when inflation is low and when prices are largely falling because of good competition, innovation, and management, wages are also going to keep steady. This does not mean that wage earners aren't better off, even based only on the buying power of their earnings. Combine this with the increasing value of their investments, and class warfare becomes a myth. As Thomas Sowell of the Hoover Institution has stressed, in America the poor tend to remain so for about five years, so the poor keep changing, just as one would expect in a volatile, dynamic economic culture. Imagine how much better things could be without any government meddling at all.

Indeed, there is a strong prospect of growing class warfare as a result of government fiddling with the economy. Governments create the permanent welfare class, making it tolerable to remain at the lowest rung of the economic ladder for millions of people. Subsidization of failing businesses, support for extravagant big business ventures such as overseas advertising—all these tend to fix people in various spots on the economic continuum.

The problem isn't, then, with free markets spawning class warfare between the rich and the poor. In the free market, the rich and poor exchange their positions constantly, repeatedly, in an ongoing competition where no legal protection exists for the rich nor are there any incentives to remain poor. Indeed, there is no evidence of two distinct classes in a free market society. Furthermore, the various places people occupy on the economic ladder are pretty much earned, with only a little influence from luck and mishap.

It is government intervention that fixes people's economic position, and those who would remedy the inequalities of capitalism by the regimentation of the welfare state and socialism are killing the only chance people have for prosperity: free trade.

11

INDIVIDUAL RIGHTS, DEMOCRACY, AND GOVERNMENT DEBT

Taxation without representation is tyranny.

—James Otis

There is always some talk about the national debt. It is the subject of much campaign rhetoric, of course. Containing it has been something of a priority to political leaders, although some have also pooh-poohed the need for this since, as they have claimed, the government's being in debt means that we owe money to ourselves and surely there is nothing wrong with that!

Serious economists who discuss government debts have tended to argue mostly about whether it is good or bad public finance policy. Some claim that a balanced budget will make the government stronger and provide it with greater confidence that it now has in the bond markets—so it can raise money with greater ease when it needs to. Some supply-siders even associate a balanced budget with the prospect of greater tax revenues in response to budgetary discipline and stability as well as the resulting higher economic activity.

It is the nature of economic science that it will tend to focus on the macroeconomic picture and the overall social results of various public policies, but this overlooks an issue that would seem to belong on anyone's mind who wants to assess public policy in terms of whether it is consistent with certain broader economic ideals or principles. After all, that is a part of how many other policies are evaluated when it comes to such aspects of community life such as crime control, education, or welfare policy.

For example, one point of judicial review is to check, when presented with a challenge, whether a given public policy— including government macro-economic—squares with the basic principles of the society. What is the point of such a check? To see if emerging policies remain consistent with the fundamental principles of the United States or whether some kind of betrayal is in the offing. The reasonable assumption in the case of the United States is that those principles have a great deal going for them, compared with other live options that might guide public policy.

It is especially important to keep this in mind when it comes to economic policy forged by various governmental bodies since, as I have already suggested, such policy tends to be guided by purely utilitarian considerations, namely, whether its results benefit the country at large. Social cost-benefit analysis is inherently utilitarian in character: Will some environmental regulations cost too many jobs? Will a certain trade policy take too many jobs from Americans or increase them? That some individuals may be hurt by the policies in question is not of great concern to the policy forgers.

But the country's laws, starting with those bearing on crime all the way to those on international relations, are always subject to scrutiny on the basis of how individual citizens are affected. If a plant is granted a license to pollute because doing otherwise will have an adverse impact on overall employment but some innocent individuals in the neighborhood will suffer, this is a problem for a country, especially one such as ours in which individual rights have played such an important role.

Not even democratic rule survives a review based on individual rights, since allowing democracy full range is to run the risk of hurting innocent individuals. It courts danger even to democracy itself since one could invalidate the democratic process by a democratic vote unless that process is itself limited in its scope.

Not all the principles of a country are explicitly stated in its basic documents—for example, in the U.S. Constitution. It is also important to reflect upon how current policy lines up with some of the principles that are sound and, moreover, were clearly on the minds of the those who founded the country but didn't get expressed in legal documents. Even the U.S. Constitution alerts us to this need in the Ninth Amendment, the purpose of which is, sadly, such a mystery to many, including those in the field of jurisprudence.

One such basic yet unofficial principle on the minds of the founders and framers is an idea articulated by James Otis. It was actually, as one report put it, "the guide and watchword of all the friends of liberty" at the time of the American Revolution, namely, that there must be no taxation without representation!

The meaning of this idea is clear enough: If a person is going to be required to contribute his or her livelihood to the maintenance of our political order, that person, unless a criminal or someone loyal to some foreign nation, must be included among the voters who have a say in how the country is going to be run. Why? Because it is only just that one should have a say about something one must pay for out of one's life's earnings. Anything else would make taxation—bad enough as it is—in no way different from outright theft. In this way, some semblance of morality is retained in the taxation process by including the taxed parties in the decision making concerning how the funds extracted from them will be spent.

In the context of the history of taxation, this is a vast improvement over what that institution used to involve, namely, simply seizing people's earnings and using them as the lord and master saw fit.

Yet in our time any measure of public debt puts into grave doubt whether the United States is loyal to the idea of "no taxation without representation." Are we reverting to an era when people were taxed and then no one bothered to learn what they would want their money spent on? That was an era, one might recall, when people living in a country were regarded as subjects, not as sovereign citizens. Sovereignty belonged only to the state or the king.

One of the tenets of a democratic society is to ensure that the sovereignty of every citizen is respected, honored, and protected. The financing of public programs from a large national debt, which is to be paid back by citizens who aren't old enough to vote or who aren't even born yet, undercuts this democratic ideal. It is, thus, a serious regression to an age when the individual purposes of citizens didn't matter, when consent of the governed was of no importance.

In our day this may not be as blatant as in the past, but with the funding of public programs from a huge debt it comes mighty close to it. We are, to put it bluntly, placing members of future generations of Americans into involuntary servitude, not even giving them the chance to campaign and vote against programs we expect them to pay for.

There are lots of complicated economic debates surrounding the issue of whether a country's public policies should be heavily financed from borrowed funds, but the idea that there ought to be no taxation unless those taxed are properly represented within government is crucial and worthy of a national debate. In a sense, it is the concession paid by the American founders to the point that in a truly free society taxation is an anomaly. Where there is no monarch who owns the realm, it is plain extortion to coerce citizens to pay for services for which they have not asked. If, however, they are well represented in the allocation of the funds collected through taxes, then taxation will come to resemble its replacement, namely, voluntary fees paid for services.

It would elevate the quality of contemporary political discussion if the principle involved here were to become a subject of serious focus. It might even lead to a serious debate about the nature of taxation itself.

12

EXPLORING EXTREME
VIOLENCE (TORTURE)

The concept of violence is often used vaguely in ordinary discourse. If we hear of violence in Burma, for example, it is unclear whether what occurred is general mayhem, a clash between aggressive and innocent persons, or ongoing physical conflict between groups of people vying for political power and advantage. Violence undertaken by people involves the use of force in the accomplishment of some goal. An army can attack with extreme violence, even when its attack is fully justified (say, against Hitler's military forces in Italy). A hoodlum can act with great violence toward his victim. On the other hand, a victim can react violently to being threatened with harm—for example, after being told, at the point of a gun, to hand over his wallet, the victim might suddenly erupt into fierce violence and overpower the hoodlum.

Violence is not confined to human behavior. A tiger can attack its prey violently. Even inanimate objects can participate in violence—as in a violent storm or a violent explosion.

Violence, then, is at first neutral, with no clear moral quality attendant to it. Both criminals and the best of law enforcers can engage in violent behavior. To know where right and justice lie, more would seem to be required than simply knowing of the violence that has occurred between human beings. Thus when the violence is between two equally corrupt parties, such as gangs, or dictatorial political forces (for example, in Haiti), the mere presence of violence can clearly be ascertained without any assessment of its justifiability.

But when we ask whether any justification of violence is possible—or, more specifically, whether it may ever be legitimate in the context of a truly just legal system—violence is viewed as the deliberate use of excessive or even extreme force by human beings upon human beings. Torture would be a clear candidate for extreme violence used by some on others. There is little doubt that physical torture is an instance of violence, and there is no doubt that the justifiability of such violence is in serious question. In most civilized legal codes, torture is outlawed. This instance of violence seems generally to be unjustifiable and illegal.

Yet one can easily conceive of circumstances that would tend to make some extreme violence morally justifiable. Suppose that a little girl is kidnapped by two known child molesters and murderers and one of these has been caught while the other is still at large with the child. Suppose also that it is known that the captured kidnapper-molester-murderer knows where his partner is hiding with the child but does not want to yield the information, fearing future reprisals. Is it so incredible to contemplate that the captured kidnapper-molester-murderer ought to be tortured so as to gain the chance to rescue the innocent victim still in the grasp of his partner? If the child were one's own beloved four-year-old daughter and one had to make the decision irrespective of any legal supervision—for example, in some state-of-nature situation—the prospect of torture would not be at all morally incredible.

But from all this are we to conclude that at least in some circumstances, torture is morally justifiable? If so, have we legitimated a case of violence? Then we could establish, by reference to paradigm cases, that violence may at times be legitimate. Before we leap to the conclusion just suggested, it will be useful to consider the case imagined in further detail.

For one thing, have I not painted the situation in such a fashion that the torture involved against the captive kidnapper-molester-murderer amounts to a kind of retaliatory violence? In short, have I not loaded that case so that we are not actually considering the legitimization of violence in the more difficult sense, namely, when it is unprovoked by violence initiated upon someone? In my example, we are dealing with a violent response against someone who has committed violence and has not yet been punished for it. Wouldn't the case be more difficult and to the point if we had someone who knows where the kidnapper is hiding the child but had no part in the kidnapping and simply does not cooperate, perhaps for fear of retaliation from the kidnappers? It is less credible in such a case that we ought to torture the uncooperative witness—indeed, it seems quite unlikely that it could be justified.

Yet we can imagine a case where the stakes are even greater than rescuing an innocent child from almost certain molestation and murder. What if a witness just happened to know where a mad bomber is hiding and getting ready to blow up an entire city? For unfathomable reasons—fear, cowardice, moral blindness, general nihilism, or despondency—the witness will not produce the testimony needed to prevent the bombing. Would we then permit violence (for example, torture) to secure the information? It is now more credible to argue that we would. Yet here, too, the witness may be guilty of something to begin with—for example, being silent in the face of some innocent people's mistreatment—so again our actions must be understood in that context. The witness very probably is seriously at fault for not mustering the willingness to report on the bomber and thus verges on becoming an accessory after the fact. (Being an accessory after the fact counts as a serious charge in the criminal laws of most societies.)

Underlying the credibility of torture in each case I have been discussing seems to be a theory of value, namely, the view that saving innocent human life—and especially great numbers of innocent human lives—would justify extreme actions, especially when the target of the extreme measure is in some ways implicated. Yet that does not tell the whole story.

If we could rescue thousands by murdering or torturing just a few who have no complicity in the danger facing the thousands, somehow the credibility I have been suggesting would vanish. What is necessary is some measure of complicity. Thus, when a witness *ought to* cooperate with us but chooses not to, we hold this against her, morally speaking, and that lends credibility to the suggestion that violence might be committed against her. I have already noted that the complicity is akin to being accessory to a crime. But it might be understood also in witnesses in a trial; if they are subpoenaed and refuse to testify, they are in contempt of court and subject to sanctions.

What this may allow us to conclude is that torture may indeed be morally justified at times, but only if it is highly probable or demonstrable that the party to experience the torture is guilty of dastardly conduct, the goal of the torturer is very worthy, and it appears that the goal cannot be achieved without the torture.

Now, in these cases the kind of violence we are considering inflicting on the guilty parties is of a particularly excessive type—torture. We would normally grant that we may retaliate forcibly when force is applied against innocent persons, "innocent" meaning here that the person is not known to be culpably involved in any wrongdoing that might be met with violence. We usually would not accept that retaliatory force be of the kind represented by torture. In the cases I have discussed, however, it is just such quasi-retaliatory force that seems to be justified. I say "quasi-retaliatory" because in the cases considered, the torture clearly does not have the purpose *merely* of retaliating against some violent wrongdoing. It also has the purpose of obtaining information.

However, because the parties upon whom the torture would be inflicted are guilty of—or at least complicit in shielding—a kind of violent wrongdoing that has (in a way) brought it about that the information must be secured, the type of more-than-strictly-retaliatory violence involved does appear to be justified under the circumstances. In some sense, we may take it that given the situation, the parties—by the logic of their conduct—asked for the torture, given that *that* is the *best* way to rescue their victims. So although retaliation is not the key issue, there is a similar quid pro quo involved. If torture is the best way to counter what the guilty parties have done, torture it shall be.

Again, all this applies thus far only to what an individual might be morally justified in doing. We turn now to the distinct question of whether the moral justifiability of extreme violence (for example, torture) informs us in any definitive fashion about the lawfulness of such extreme violence in a just legal system.

When a legal system is unjust, depending on the degree of injustice, certain degrees of violence may have to be legally tolerated—for example, when it is clearly shown that the violence was a singular means of responding to the injustice in question. But since the issue here is whether extreme violence is ever to be legally justified, we are involved in a prelegal discussion, one that would have to be conducted with reference to the conceptualization of a just legal system. In other words, the question we face here is whether extreme violence of the sort represented by torture could ever be a legitimate part of a just legal system. The sorts of questions that arise in connection with actual cases, whether historical or contemporary, would arise logically only after we have handled the present general topic.

Let us imagine that the suspected or alleged kidnapper captured in the case above is now in the hands of the police. He still refuses to inform on his partner and thus to help save the child from molestation and murder. Should the legal system of a society permit the police to employ the extreme violence of torture to obtain the needed information? (Another important issue is that evidence extracted through the use of torture is considered tainted and thus inadmissible. Therefore, although they would rescue the child, the case may not be successful in court and the criminals might go free.)

Sometimes acts may be morally justified even if the law should, as a matter of its generality, forbid it. For example, trespassing is generally illegal, but in certain cases one ought to trespass—for example, if one needs to do so in order to rescue an injured child or perhaps even an animal. Because of such cases, however, the law of trespass need not be rescinded or nullified. Rather, courts can practice what I will call, for lack of a better term, judicial discretion—basically, the power to decide in extraordinary fashion, based on special circumstances—as they sometimes do now. To use an even more drastic example, the Donner Party's actions do not show that cannibalism is or should be legitimate, only that the law does not in every conceivable case go the distance of punishing it.

One might, of course, claim that once the court is involved in such a case, any ruling, however unusual, would have the force of law behind it. Even a presidential pardon is a legal instrument. This is granted in the present discussion, but it is also clear that although the law is predominantly general, yielding implications for similar instances, when judges invoke the instrument of what I have called judicial discretion, they recognize the extraordinary nature of the case and intend to place it into a unique category.

From these considerations, it can now be noted that even though individual human beings sometimes morally ought to or may commit extreme violence such as torture, it does not yet follow that such violence ought to be sanctioned by the law of a just human community. In other words, although the moral permissibility of extreme violence need not always be denied, this does not establish its legal permissibility.

So there are actions that police officers might justifiably undertake without such actions being justified in the law. They might act as private individuals—as do attorneys and educators and physicians—even while they normally occupy their professional roles. When a police officer takes a turn or two at some game with local youths, this is not conduct in the line of duty! When an educator gives some helpful advice to a student about how to deal with parents, that again goes beyond pedagogy.

Similarly, it is possible that a police officer dealing with a suspect ought to circumvent his or her official role and do certain things—harsh or kind—that are not strictly in line with his or her duty. His or her superiors might, of course, have to act against the officer per the requirements of their office. If this is granted, we can appreciate that although it is credible that even a police officer ought to employ extreme violence in certain circumstances, it does not follow from this that the law—the general principles guiding the conduct of the officer qua officer—ought to sanction such violence.

Why might it be categorically wrong for the law to sanction extreme violence? My initial answer to this question relies on our appreciation of the concept of due process.

The use of extreme violence by officers of the legal system subverts due process of law. I have in mind not simply due process in its purely procedural sense. Such an idea of due process can be complied with by merely following something akin to the democratic process; that is, as long as the electoral process—or whatever other method of lawmaking is practiced— of a society is not abrogated, due process of law is taken to be upheld. But this is too weak, as we can glean from how Adolf Hitler wrested power by way of the quasi-democratic process emanating from the Weimar Republic that preceded the Third Reich.

I have in mind the substantive kind of due process, whereby certain principles of justice are assumed to hold and need to be adhered to in order to achieve lawfulness. I am not going to involve myself here with a defense and elaboration of the relevant principles of justice or with the attendant controversy between natural and positive law doctrines. What I would like to do is merely to call attention to certain familiar ideas of substantive due process—for example, the right not to incriminate oneself in the course of a judicial process; the placing of the onus of proof in criminal trials; and the proscription against prior restraint in at least some of the criminal law.

Admittedly, these are all parts of the substantive due process of the kind of legal system we find in our largely classical-liberal political tradition. *They are by no means politically neutral!* They rely for their credibility on certain assumptions concerning the inviolability of certain rights or of innocent persons, which itself assumes a conception of a limited type of (legal) innocence, namely, that one has not violated another's rights. As I noted, though, I am not going to be able to go into this in detail.

Suffice it to say that if there is anything to these considerations—and one would assume that the concern with legitimating violence already presupposes some idea of individual rights and their inviolability—one can begin to appreciate why the legal system of a society that takes them seriously should not legally sanction the use of extreme violence, such as torture. Such a system is committed to treating everyone as *not legally guilty* unless proved so under the careful supervision of a court of law where rules of evidence and so forth are adhered to as closely as is practically possible. The reason for this is that within the philosophical tradition underlying such a legal system, individuals are regarded as normally capable of making free choices. If we assume that persons are, on the contrary, passive patients and not free agents, then this assumption would have to be rejected, but then it is entirely unclear what we would substitute so as to still have a legal system other than some form of elitism that treats some citizens as free agents and others as passive patients.

Accordingly, in a system wherein all citizens are regarded as having an equal standing under the law—whether they be rich or poor, beautiful or ugly, black or brown, men or women—no one may be treated as if he or she were not a free agent or as if he or she were already convicted of a crime and, most relevantly for our purposes, *subject to punishment.*

For this reason I would conclude that despite the *moral* justifiability of some uses of extreme violence, such as torture, for individual cases, the law of a just human community that takes the tradition of individual rights seriously should not sanction such conduct. It should be held illegal. This does not mean that no one should ever engage in such conduct, only that the law should not construe it as justifiable, especially in the course of the administration of justice. If torture does come to the attention of the legal authorities, it must be prosecuted, although in extreme cases the vehicle of a pardon could signal the understanding of an exceptional situation.

13

THE NORMS OF
GOVERNMENT INTERVENTION

Sometimes we suffer unexpected setbacks in life, even calamities, and the basic question to face is how to prepare for and cope with these. Of course, the answers will often be fitted to those who ask it and cannot be expected to be the same for all.

Some of us need insurance, others investment, and others, like insurance companies, reinsurance. Sometimes we need to dip into savings, at other times we get a loan or sell something so that we can buy emergency goods to recover from the problem. Now and then, nothing much will work.

In a free society, which we sadly only approximate in the United States, everyone would be on notice to arrange for emergencies. Indeed, various businesses and charities would flourish from our decision to make plans and to help those who could turn out to be in dire straits. This is not different from how people in a free society, and even in one that's only semi-free, meet other needs they have. The idea is to find millions of solutions except ones that violate rights! Desperation is no excuse for breaches of morality and justice.

It is no news, of course, that when difficulties arise in our lives, the temptation is strong for some of us to abandon loyalty to our principles. It is when a marriage is facing problems that people are tempted to become adulterers. It's when they are poor that they consider that perhaps a little theft or burglary could be the answer to their problems. It is when we are afraid of the truth that lying looks attractive to us.

So why would it be surprising that after a major upheaval like that brought to America's shores on September 11, 2001, people who have already been accustomed to do it in ordinary circumstances now run to government for "help"?

No, they aren't asking for bona fide help. What government does usually is to use its legal power of arms to force others to come up with the money—often even against unborn members of future generations who cannot defend themselves even via the rather risky democratic method. They cannot vote against the people who would place them into debt. This is a notorious case of taxation without representation, something that even our semi-free country was supposed to reject but perpetrates against minors who work and against the yet unborn who will grow up owing a lot of taxes!

What government does when it bails us out is to take other people's resources and provide them to some who are in special need—or simply have enough political clout. Genuine help, however, is the contributions made by millions who can afford it, including the numerous big and small business corporations that have given—not stolen and then transferred—funds to the hard-hit victims and their families.

That is what helping means among free men and women, and what President George W. Bush and others in Washington and in the country's media are planning and urging be done is but another extension of a basically unjust public policy.

The fact is that however much of an emergency one faces, it should never be made into public policy to abandon the basic principles of a free society: the respect and protection of our unalienable individual rights to what belongs to us and the need to obtain support from us with our consent. Government's role should not change even when the chips are down—it should still be primarily concerned with securing our rights.

What political leaders can do to contribute to recovery is, first, to dig into their own wallets and be generous and charitable with their own money and, second, urge us through their easy access to the media to find ways to help ourselves and others.

But no, sadly what is on the minds of most politicians and pundits is how to redistribute resources at the point of gun, something that isn't generous, isn't charitable, and doesn't qualify as help. Instead it helps most people to be deluded to think that perhaps something can come from nothing, that government is almighty after all, and that violating the basic principles of life is the way to cope with emergencies. In fact, the only just approach for a government is to uphold the principles of a free society come hell or high water!

This isn't all that different from how we actually live most of the time in our private lives—when even serious problems arise, when we are in special need, we do not rob our next-door neighbor or dump our problems on unwilling others, but double up our own efforts and reach out for support from those who will give it of their own free choice.

So we can ask, "What if a tornado hits? What if a lot of tornadoes hit?" The free society is supposed to be governed with an eye to securing the rights to life, liberty, and the pursuit of happiness. Briefly, a free society rests on the fact that adult human beings at all times, in all places, are first and foremost sovereign individuals with the capacity for self-rule, for self-directedness. This capacity is a defining attribute of human beings, not merely specific to certain cultures, as some critics of classical liberalism would have it. An adult human being needs to learn and is capable of learning how to live and flourish independently. Any community worthy of being considered a human one must accommodate this fact about us. Yes, we are also social beings, but not just any kind of society will do our individuality justice. The novelty of the American political vision, however ill or well realized it has been in America's history, is its affirmation of the sovereignty of individuals and its establishment of a legal order in which this sovereignty is to be secured, protected, and maintained.

But what do we do when disaster strikes? Natural calamities—for example, earthquakes, floods, tidal waves, hurricanes, tornadoes, and typhoons—seem to warrant an expansion of governmental authority beyond what a free society would sanction. Government has indeed habitually stepped in with all sorts of measures whenever and wherever disasters have struck. Flood control measures are usually deemed to be its business. Few batted an eye even when the U.S. Army was called out to battle Hurricane Andrew in Florida. What is government for if not to come to the aid of citizens in such circumstances?[1]

Even in personal affairs, using physical force can sometimes be justifiable—for example, when one needs to yank an unsuspecting person from the path of imminent deadly danger. As John Stuart Mill argued, physically blocking someone from stepping on to a collapsing bridge is justified even in the context of adhering to the basic principles of individual liberty and minimal government.

Yet as Robert Higgs (in *Crisis and Leviathan*) and others have shown, it is nearly impossible to reestablish limits on government once it has acquired the legal authority to expand its powers for the sake of handling emergencies. In the law and in the making of public policy, precedent counts for a great deal; there is a slippery slope here. Once an approach is legitimized, extensions of power beyond the particular and special areas originally intended are almost inevitable. The definition of what constitutes an eligible emergency tends to broaden. Eventually, no dire need whatever can be neglected by lawmakers. What might slow or reverse such encroachment is a change of heart, some fear of going too far, or the like. Once the logic of intervening in a particular special case has been established, however, it is difficult to offer a persuasive rationale for declining to apply the same logic to similar cases—unless the legitimacy of the original intervention itself is challenged. As a result, most "temporary powers" assumed by government remain part of its permanent repertoire.

Consider gun control legislation. The Second Amendment to the U.S. Constitution was undermined early on in our legislative history. Now, especially in the wake of tragic shootings—at schools, restaurants, post offices, and amusement parks—it has become harder and harder to raise principled objections against more and more restrictions on the right of self-defense. The citizenry demands it, and the politicians have precedents.

Such decline and fall of political principles serve to underscore the integrity of those principles. They can't normally be violated, even a little, with impunity; minor incursions tend to snowball, especially when hallowed in law. Even so, a powerful tradition of political thinking challenges the value of such integrity. In contemporary American politics and, indeed, around the world, it is often deemed a good thing to be "flexible." Principled politics is dismissed by many sophisticated thinkers as "mere ideology." Instead of ideology, they argue, we should embrace pragmatism.

The term *ideology* is burdened by a number of pejorative connotations, often imported into the implicit definition of the term. For example, there is Marx's claim that principled economic and political thinking can be nothing but rationalization for class interest (with his own economic and political thinking somehow granted exemption from this indictment, however). Those who defend a substantially laissez-faire, free market system—like Adam Smith and David Ricardo—are, by Marx's view, merely doing so to promote the class interest of capitalists, wealthy people served by such a system. Their principled advocacy amounts to nothing more than special pleading.

Ideology is also supposed to be the hobbyhorse of the simplistic thinker, inclining one to provide knee-jerk solutions to complex problems. This is the charge lodged against those who would apply political principles to judge what public officials ought to do in particular cases. Presumably, the resort to principle allows one, and perhaps even encourages one, to ignore details of the specific context at hand.

An objective definition of ideology (i.e., a definition that doesn't import various charges against believers in a particular ideology) might be *a set of political values and doctrines advanced in support of a particular social-political system*. The definition says nothing about what those values and doctrines might be or whether their justification of a particular social system is successful. That has to be evaluated independently; the sheer fact of possessing a belief cannot be taken as proof of the falsehood or disingenuousness of that belief. (It may well be that if even a capitalist says two plus two is four, it really is four.) To be sure, even the critics of ideology have ideologies of their own. Of course, theirs is usually construed as being the result of long and hard thinking and observations about community life, productive of sound judgments and evaluations; it's the other guy with the other ideology who is the thoughtless propagandist for rigid and unworkable answers.

We don't have to choose between facts-of-the-case and principles-that-govern, however. Politics, in fact, requires both principled thinking and proper flexibility in applying those principles to the relevant context.

Just as in our personal lives, in politics and law we need basic ideas that serve as the foundation for understanding how human communities ought to function, and we need to practice and abide by those ideas. If they're valid, we ought not ignore them when the tough cases come along, sacrificing the long-term benefits of principled action for the sake of short-term convenience. Yet it is also vital that cases be considered in light of the detailed facts, many of which may be new and might even require some modification of the principles that guide legal decision making. New ways of communicating, new religious movements, and new forms of artistic expression all require the application of familiar principles (such as those embodied in the First Amendment) in imaginative yet consistent ways.

Certainly, it is unrealistic to expect that either flexible case-by-case assessment alone, or rigid and unreflective application of principles alone, could be sufficient to formulate sound public policy. The dogmatic approach is largely eschewed by prominent contemporary political intellectuals. However, many do regard every problem as unique, thus fostering public policies and legal decisions that do not in practice conform to any basic principles (except perhaps the principle of pragmatism itself).

As a result, those who administer public policy and law more and more have become the ultimate arbiters of what will be acceptable public policy. That, in turn, is defeating the ideal of the rule of law, the only reasonable alternative to the rule of arbitrary human will, whether of a majority, a king, or a single ruling party. The rule of law allows everyone to participate in the assessment of public policy and legal decision making; we can all evaluate whether our policy and lawmakers are doing the right thing by reference to a knowable, objective standard. If no principles apply, then anything goes. Usually, the most emotionally appealing choice of the moment is accepted, which means that those who are most adept at expressing and manipulating emotions—the demagogues—are the ones who tend to carry the day. In emergencies, especially massive emergencies that have a wide impact on a society, the opportunities for such demagoguery abound.

Is the championing of flexibility a good idea? Is it really a valid approach to politics and lawmaking? A hint that it might not be is provided by the fact that even many pragmatists recoil from their own approach when they think that the values at stake are too important to be forsaken even a little. No self-respecting moral theorist would propose that when a man forces a women to have sex with him, the moral and legal status of the act should be mulled anew with each case. Instead, everyone accepts the principle that a person has the right to choose with whom he or she will have sex and thus that any clear violation of this right is grounds for sanction. But this is the opposite of being pragmatically flexible without regard for principle.

Imagine how members of a jury in a rape case might deliberate if they were eager to be flexible and avoid being "rigid." They would steer clear of blind obedience to "dogmatic" principles—such as the need to respect the rights of the victim or to be objective about the evidence for the guilt of the defendant. Rather, the jurors would attend to such emotionally resonant considerations as whether the perpetrator is a nice person, has appealing attributes, serves the community vigilantly, promotes economic prosperity, paints, or throws a football well. The distress of the victim may or may not enter into such a calculus. After all, what if the victim has a checkered past, is rude to the bailiff, or just doesn't emote well on the stand? By the standard of pragmatic flexibility, basing decisions on such factors may well be unimpeachable. By contrast, a principled approach would not gainsay the fact that it is a violation of basic human rights to rape someone or the fact that determining the guilt of the defendant on this score is the only purpose of the proceedings.

Is being principled "mere ideology"? Is it "simplistic"? Is it deficient in appropriate flexibility? No. Nor would it be simplistically ideological and excessively rigid to judge various other social matters by reference to certain tried and true principles, ones we have learned of over the many years of human experience with community life.

Thus, for example, when someone objects to government intrusion in the marketplace, regarding it as a violation of our economic freedom, this objection is grounded in arguably well-developed and well-established principled thinking about public economic policy. Similarly, to criticize restraint of trade because it violates private property rights and freedom of contract is no less based on tried and true principles—not as they apply to one's sovereignty over sexual matters, but as they apply to one's sovereignty over economic matters.

If we accept the validity and force of moral principles in every case that the principles legitimately govern, there would be no basis for excusing lying, cheating, fraud, rape, murder, assault, kidnapping, or any of the other myriad ways people can damage their fellows. In politics, no less so than in ethics or morality, general principles come into play as we evaluate how people conduct themselves. It is not a matter of whether we need principles, only of which principles we in fact need.

Principles are tested by hard cases. Despite the temptation to abandon the principle of limited government when it comes to calamities, we might do well to encourage the development of institutions that meet the problems without the involvement of the government (private insurance policies are one such institution). Of course, the temptation to use government power is difficult to resist, and it is legitimate to ask whether the use of government power in such cases can ever be proper and consistent with the ideal of limited government or must always generate that slippery slope.

We are familiar with the hazards of the slippery slope in our own personal lives. If a man hits his child in some alleged emergency, the very act of doing so may render him more amenable to smacking the kid under more typical circumstances. Slapping someone who is hysterical may make it easier to slap someone who is only very upset, recalcitrant, annoying, or just too slow fetching the beer from the refrigerator. Similarly, a "minor" breach of trust can beget more of the same, a little white lie here and there can beget lying as a routine, and so forth. Moral habits promote a principled course of action even in cases when bending or breaking the principle might not seem too harmful to other parties or to our own integrity. On the other hand, granting ourselves "reasonable" exceptions tends to weaken our moral habits; as we seek to rationalize past action, differences of kind tend to devolve into differences of degree. Each new exception provides the precedent for the next, until we lose our principles altogether and doing what is right becomes a matter of happenstance and mood rather than of loyalty to enduring values.

The same is true of public action. When citizens of a country delegate to government, by means of democratic and judicial processes, the power to forge paternalistic public policies like banning drug abuse, imposing censorship, and restraining undesirable and supporting desirable trade, the bureaucratic and police actions increasingly rely on the kind of violence and intrusiveness that no free citizenry ought to experience or foster. And the bureaucrats and the police officers tell themselves, no doubt, that what they're doing is perfectly just and right.

Consider, for starters, that when no one complains about a crime—because it is not perpetrated against someone but rather because it involves breaking a paternalistic law—to even detect the "crime" requires methods that are usually invasive. Instead of charges being brought by wronged parties, the dubious means that lead to prosecution include phone tapping, snooping, anonymous reporting, and undercover work. Thus the role of the police shifts from protection and peacekeeping to supervision, regimentation, and reprimand. No wonder, then, that officers of the law are often caught brutalizing suspects instead of merely apprehending them. Under a paternalistic regime, their goals have multiplied, and thus the means they see as necessary to achieving those goals multiply too.

The same general danger of corrupting a free society's system of laws may arise when government is called upon to deal with calamities. There is the perception, of course, that in such circumstances the superior powers of government are indispensable, given the immediateness of the danger. The immediate benefits—a life saved by a marine—are evident. Yet the dangers of extensive involvement by legal authority in the handling of nonjudicial problems are no less evident, even if they are less immediate in their impact.

14

DEMOCRACY, FOREIGN AFFAIRS, AND MILITARY EXPANSION

What are the standards by which the foreign policy and military affairs of a free society ought to be conducted?

In an age when government is so often tempted to expand its powers—and so often does—every citizen should give some thought to this question. The democratic character of our society is not a sufficient safeguard against abuse of governmental powers either domestically or overseas.

People often think otherwise because it was American politics that introduced to the world the modern version of democracy. Ancient or Athenian democracy was only a shadow of the American system. In ancient Greece only free citizens, all of them male and none of them slaves, could participate in politics. In the United States, indeed, something similar was established after the Constitutional Convention over 200 years ago. Eventually, though, the vote was extended to every adult and slavery was abolished. Thus the ideal of full participation of the citizenry in the political process was realized.

Yet democracy is just one of America's unique contributions to politics. The constitutional protection of individual rights, involving various constraints on even democratic governmental powers, is a deeply radical bequest. These powers were, of course, ultimately backed by the democratic process, which would apply only to politics. And politics would be confined to the protection of individual rights—except that it didn't quite work out that way.

The rights spelled out in the Bill of Rights were what are referred to as negative rights, which means that we all have the right *not* to be murdered, attacked, assaulted, robbed, and so forth. To respect our rights, other people need do no more than abstain from aggressing against us. A close reading of the Bill of Rights confirms this understanding of our rights.[1]

In time, the American view of politics became corrupted. Slowly but surely, culminating in the New Deal, New Frontier, and Great Society, we began to be awarded "positive rights," rights to have this or that specific good provided to us on a silver platter.[2] Needless to say, government could secure these new "rights" only by violating the old rights. In order to be provided with social security, unemployment compensation, Medicare, food stamps, subsidies for businesses, and preservation of "national" treasures (e.g., parks, forests, and lakes), the right of persons to spend their weekly wages as they choose had to be violated.

POSITIVE RIGHTS, AGAIN

As I have noted in the Introduction to this work, positive rights have served to criticize the free society. They limit individual freedom by coercing citizens to serve others in need or goals deemed very important. It is, after all, the doctrine that supports entitlements.

To reiterate, positive rights are intended to spell out enforceable obligations we have to others and is championed by such critics of classical liberal—and today libertarian—ideas as Karl Marx on the left and Thomas Hill Green on the right. Both held the view that the state must force us all—those at least who can—to serve others, whether we like it or not. As noted before, these "rights" are special values many want to achieve under the guise of calling them rights so that governments could be understood as established so as to secure them for people at others' expense.

Positive rights theory has served statists well in America because this country was founded on a famous theory of basic human rights, the theory originally developed by the seventeenth-century English philosopher John Locke that every individual human being has the unalienable right to life, liberty, and property. We have discussed this earlier in this work.

In foreign affairs the doctrine of positive rights means, essentially, that others around the globe are entitled to be helped by Americans. Since an entitlement is something that may be legally enforced—if one has title to something, it is one's own and may be taken by force from those who happen to possess it just now—the American government may take the wealth of its citizens via taxes and hire the needed help for those abroad who are entitled to it, including military support. It may also delegate the authority to administer the delivery of that help to NATO or the United Nations. So, among other arguments, the positive rights doctrine gives support to American foreign military intervention despite the fact that by the doctrine of negative rights only defensive military action would be warranted.

There is a way to argue, somewhat plausibly, that negative rights—to life, liberty, or the pursuit of happiness, for example—imply positive rights, namely, to the protection of negative rights, a protection that is surely a kind of service. Several defenders of positive rights have argued this way.[3]

However, first such protection presupposes the existence of negative rights that need the protection, so in any case negative rights are prior to positive rights, even if the latter do exist. And, so as to obtain the protection, those who provide it need to be paid and those for whom the protection is provided must consent to be given the protection. So the positive rights are contractual, parasitic on the prior exercise of negative rights (in this case, to engage in consenting to be governed or protected in one's negative rights).

THE OBJECTIVITY OF BONA FIDE RIGHTS

Now, it is important that basic negative rights are objective principles of human social life; otherwise, if they were no more than our preferences, there would be no end of conflict between our rights. Indeed, there are many conservatives who have some sympathy for elements of classical liberalism, including John Locke's views, and who see rights the same way. They embrace the basic view of Thomas Hobbes and David Hume that an assertion of a right, for example, to private property, is nothing but a preference for owning something and as such it could be in conflict with some other right, for example, another person's similar preference to own something. The reason for this is that for these theorists these assertions are, in the last analysis, no more than expressions of private or collective preferences. Many economists view matters this way, even as they try to oppose the view that we have positive rights or entitlements.

So both some conservatives who deny that rights are natural and modern statists who believe in the existence of positive rights find themselves with the very unhappy situation that perfectly normal claims to having certain rights are usually in conflict. Governments, therefore, cannot just protect our rights but must pit some rights against other rights. Instead of government having the task of "securing these rights," government is supposed to invoke some standard apart from our rights by which to tell which and whose rights should get protection.

It needs repeating, I believe, that when countries across the globe are being judged, the issue is which are comparatively best, not the best that is possible. This way the greater merits of certain political communities may be recognized even in the face of their violation of our basic rights. As noted already, in personal relations we can distinguish between major and minor instances of rights violation. We are just as capable of recognizing a community that is corrupt, or one that is only confused and messy, or again one that nearly meets standards of justice, namely basic human rights. That is roughly how Amnesty International and other human rights watch groups proceed as they issue their reports on the regimes around the globe. We need to aim to apply these standards more strictly and precisely, especially as we evaluate the laws and public policies of our own country.

It would behoove us all to make sure that the doctrine of positive rights receives what it deserves: precise exposition by and a carefully articulated and unmerciful lambaste from us. With its refutation, the more humane idea that we have certain moral responsibilities—of generosity, kindness, consideration of others, and charity toward others that we ought freely choose to carry out—will gain greater impact on our society, thereby fostering the solution of problems that the advocates of positive rights only pretend to tackle, however benign their intentions may be.

It is especially important to keep in mind the perils of positive rights theory when it comes to foreign affairs, given how massive the entanglement in foreign conflicts positive rights would imply and how much a drain that would be on the lives and properties of those who would be legally required to provide the support needed.

BLOATED DEMOCRACY

The democratic process today includes a wide range of participants and a wide scope of political decision making, including pertaining to what positive rights will be honored. Since positive rights specify entitlements to services and resources that are scarce, democracy must handle the troublesome task of which of such alleged rights are to be secured by government. Furthermore, realms that are in fact nongovernmental or "private" and should be rights-protected are now susceptible to invasion by the realm of politics. Members of interest groups large enough to influence those in power could demand their share of the proceeds.

As a result of what democracy means in the American political context, it is now nearly impossible to make the case for democratic politics in its original and narrower scope. Yet it may be that when it comes to contemporary foreign policy, the dangers of unfettered expansion of that scope can be given some bite.

DEMOCRACY IN A MULTICULTURAL SOCIETY

America is a pluralistic society. Nearly every nation and group from abroad has "sent" some of its members to this country. The loyalties of these citizens have not always been transferred to their new homeland, nor has our political culture urged such a change, given that this bloated version of democracy does not limit at all what people may root for at the polling booth. There is, thus, a contradictory pluralism of political demands, and this can have a destructive impact on foreign policy.

For example, when it comes to the mess in the Balkans, immigrants from Bosnia have urged our government to fight on the side of Bosnia, while those from Serbian regions demanded that the Serbs be assisted. African Americans champion various foreign policy projects in South Africa, Somalia, or Ethiopia. Irish, Armenian, Russian, and Jewish Americans have their own desires they would have our government satisfy.

Many of these objectives are perfectly benign—such as rectifying injustices, feeding starving people, and establishing peace between fighting groups. There is, moreover, no end to such worthy goals—matched, no doubt, by many others that are less than savory.

INDIVIDUALISM AND DEMOCRACY

One reason for the great diversity of benign goals is that human beings differ from each other significantly, so that what is of benefit for some may not be for others. Hardly any of these objectives are universally valid for every human being, not to mention every American citizen. In short, not all the matters that come up for public discussion are everyone's concern.

Yet, because of our bloated democracy, every one of these group concerns is thrust upon the shoulders of the entire nation willy-nilly. Today's headlines confirm the fact starkly. The government of the United States is being egged on to get involved in nearly every international conflict or crisis. This usually means that America's armed forces are being urged not only to do what they are sworn to do—defend our citizenry from foreign aggressors—but to be not only the policeman but the social worker of nearly every region of the globe.

If government's function, however, is to protect individual negative rights, there is no systematic danger of pitting groups against groups since governments will not redistribute scarce resources but enforce laws that demand abstinence from the use of force. If force, however, is omnipresent in the task of solving social problems, quite apart from the protection of negative rights, the role of democracy will be to determine where it must be deployed. Democracy shall determine who are the beneficiaries and losers in the process of wealth—in other words, resource and services—redistribution.

In a very imaginative and alarming essay, Lt. Colonel Charles Dunlop, Jr., has argued that certain contemporary trends that involve the expansion of the use of military power are quite ominous.[4] Such a use of military force expands the role of the military in American social life to the point that the population may be inclined to entrust many of the important social tasks to the military and thus encourage the emergence of permanent martial law.

Combined with the democratic method this can encourage a kind of democratic totalitarianism, namely, by increasingly deploying government authority in all realms of social life—the war on drugs, coping with natural disasters, and so forth—as well as lending military aid to other regions of the world where such matters need to be addressed.

Perhaps this prospect, made evident in our foreign affairs, will finally persuade our citizenry to restrain our government and give democracy a job it is fit to handle.

15

WHY ABORTION IS NOT MURDER

A bortion is not necessarily murder. It is not murder if a fetus—or an "unborn child," as some would have it—is only potentially a human being and not yet actually a human being.[1] Killing such a fetus is thus no more homicide than killing a seed is murdering a flower.

I wish to spell out a view on abortion that escapes the criticisms leveled at a similar treatment of the topic, namely, Ayn Rand's. Though my own position is something of a departure from Rand's, it argues in the same spirit.

The main question involved in the abortion debate is: When does a human being, qua human being, come into existence? As Feinberg (1980: 184) poses the question:

> At what stage, if any, in the development between conception and birth do fetuses acquire the characteristic (whatever it may be) that confers on them the appropriate status to be included in the scope of the moral rule against homicide—the rule "Thou shalt not kill"? Put more tersely, at what stage, if any, of their development do fetuses become people?

This question involves many ancient, serious, and divisive philosophical topics, one for which the different schools of philosophy, religions, and moral theories have suggested diverse answers. Hindus, Aristotelians, Kantians, utilitarians, Christians of one or another denomination, and so forth identify different points of the development of the organism at which a human being comes into existence. Other disputes also arise, based on the clashing ontological and epistemological doctrines that are deployed in discussions of human nature.

In a predominantly Christian culture, the answer to questions of the sort identified by Feinberg are usually sought from the Bible, but the good book does not directly deal with this question. The Christian God commands that no one shall kill another human being, but he doesn't bother to specify exactly when a human being comes into existence.

Nevertheless, many Christian denominations have committed themselves to the view that a human being emerges into full-fledged existence at conception—notwithstanding the biological fact that, at conception, no individual organism at all exists, but only a zygote. It takes about fourteen days after conception before one or more individual embryos come into existence. Inasmuch as it is only at this point that ensoulment could occur, it is only at this point that the number of souls that can be carried in pregnancy could be determined (assuming that souls are indeed immediately awarded to the embryos once they do emerge). Theological thinking cannot resolve the issue definitively and is not persuasive to the secular mind in any case.

Secular thinking on the issue has hardly presented a uniform alternative so far. Some believe that the human being comes into existence at birth because its identity is determined by social acknowledgement of that identity. Others believe that because of the difficulty of establishing the point of full development of the embryo, we should err on the side of caution and stipulate that a human being exists from the fourteenth day after conception. Yet others hold the view, implicit in the famous U.S. Supreme Court decision *Roe v. Wade* (1973), that only after the cerebral cortex has fully developed, at about the twenty-fourth week of pregnancy, has a human being emerged. The distinctively human capacity to reason emerges as an actuality only with the development of the cerebral cortex. Prior to that point, the pregnancy involves only a *potential,* only an *undeveloped* human infant, like the caterpillar that is not yet a butterfly.

What is especially nettlesome for purposes of public policy in the United States is that the people to be governed by it hail from a great variety of traditions, cultures, and religions. By contrast, a nearly homogeneous people populates many other countries, with a preponderance of specific ethnic, religious, or racial groups making up the citizenry. Israel, Iran, and Pakistan are reasonably good examples, although even here diversity exists.

When they spoke, in the Declaration of Independence, of "all men" having been created equal, the American founders were at least implicitly aware that political communities must not be shaped so as to cater to a specific ethnic, racial, or religious group at the expense of others. The framers, in turn, created a constitution with a Bill of Rights that speaks of the rights of the people *as individuals.* They drew heavily on both the secular and faith-based political ideas of humanists like Socrates, Aristotle, and Thomas Hobbes, and Christians like John Locke; they wrote in broad enough terms so as to embrace both religious and secular interpretations of humanity's creation and nature.

Now when it comes to identifying basic laws of human communities and to whom these apply, although there is a common core of agreement across traditions and religions, there are many differences as well. Borderline cases can be especially perplexing. For some, for example, animals are owed the kind of protection of rights that nearly everyone recognizes human beings to possess. For others, the health of their children may be attended to via prayer alone and without resort to medical services. This raises questions of neglect when the child's life is in danger and might be saved by standard medicine.

U.S. constitutional law has tended to deal with such issues on the basis of principles that can apply to *all members* of the population, regardless of specific cultural tradition, religion, or ethnic origin. Accordingly, for example, whatever one's religion teaches, a child must receive ordinary medical care from his parents or guardians. The killing of a cow is not a crime, regardless of the fact that one may very sincerely believe, on religious grounds, that it is.

There are many various and contradictory beliefs about the abortion issue, too, yet we are in need of a reasonably stable approach to it that satisfies the requirement of being suitable to a diverse population in virtue of applying a few common premises based on our common humanity. I propose the following: that we not wait until a child has been born in the usual sense to consider killing it a homicide, nor that we consider it homicide to kill someone who has not yet developed, even in the slightest, the familiar distinguishing capacity of a human being—in other words, the capacity (even if not yet exercised) to think and conceptualize.

Around the twenty-fourth week of pregnancy, the biological basis for the human capacity to think develops within the fetus. At this point, if one were to abort it, one could reasonably be regarded as killing an infant human being. Prior to this stage of pregnancy, it may be well immoral to abort the fetus, but apart from the strictures of a specific religious tradition, it could not reasonably be construed as homicide.

That seems to be a most sensible approach, whatever one's own religious or philosophical orientation might be. In a society of objective law, it would be wrong to convict someone of killing a human being if by normally available means one simply *cannot* identify the victim to be a human being—but only an entity that may eventually become one. Under such circumstances, the pregnant woman's rights to life, liberty, and the pursuit of happiness must be accorded full weight and legal protection. Similarly, one cannot convict a killer of a cow or a rhesus monkey of homicide just because a certain religious or philosophical tradition would classify the killing as such.

Some have argued that the identity of a person remains constant from conception to death. They are in error. The reasons given vary, but one is of some importance here since the present discussion rests on certain Aristotelian ideas, ideas also invoked by pro-life advocates. In a recent paper, Gregory R.

Johnson and David Rasmussen write that Ayn Rand's "basically Aristotelian framework would seem an unlikely foundation for a defense of abortion on demand, for the simple reason that Catholic natural law moralists use essentially the same premises to argue that abortion on demand is murder" (Johnson and Rasmussen 2000: 246). This assertion is a tad misleading. After all, Thomas Aquinas, the quintessential Roman Catholic natural law moralist, believed that not until approximately the twenty-fourth week does a human being come into existence. That is when quickening or the life of a human being begins.[2] So at least one major Roman Catholic Aristotelian—the one whose thought would matter significantly in this debate, I should think—is closer to Rand's pro-choice position than to her pro-life critics on this topic.[3] Whether or not Aquinas or any particular Roman Catholic position is correct, my point here is simply that a broadly Aristotelian perspective does not place one ineluctably in either camp sans more specific argumentation.

Certainly, the key for this issue all depends on what constitutes a human identity. For some parties to the discussion, those animated by "identity politics," personal identity consists primarily of one's heritage—one is always most fundamentally a Welsh, Irish, Italian, Croatian, or Serb individual. For others, identity has much to do with gender, sex, or even age. But all of these are relatively superficial features, as important as they may be. Most fundamentally, one's identity consists in having in full measure those attributes that make one the kind of being that one is; and a human being is a rational animal, a being of volitional consciousness. This rational and moral capacity is the trait that most fundamentally distinguishes humans from other animals, and in virtue of which it makes sense to speak of such moral concepts as "rights" that come into play when considering an issue such as abortion.

So let us consider human development from potentiality to actuality. At conception, only a "pre-embryo" exists. As biologist F. M. Sturtevant (1994) points out, this pre-embryo "consists of the trophoblast, and a few cells comprising the embryoblast." He notes that "before day 14, when the embryo can first be said to exist, the embryoblast can develop into an embryo proper, a tumor, a hydatidiform mole, a choriocarcinoma (i.e., cancer), twins, or triplets, or, in at least two-thirds of the cases, nothing at all (due to genetic defects)." Sturtevant adds that "until the primitive streak appears at day fourteen, there is no human individual." This means that no person with an identity can exist prior to day fourteen after conception. Even after that point is reached, there is no human individual—in the sense of an organism possessing the distinctively human conceptual capacity—until much later in the fetal stage, which follows the embryonic period.

Johnson and Rasmussen object that if one "wishes to maintain that an unborn child [!] is not an actual human being, but merely a potential one, then we are entitled to ask: What kind of being is it actually?" (Johnson and Rasmussen 2000: 248).

The answer is that the identity of the being is that of a potential human being, or a human fetus (not an "unborn child," a label that begs the question). Prior to the twenty-fourth week or so, the fetus does not yet possess the capacities in light of which we assign and protect rights; these capacities are a potential. But the fetus has the potential to develop those capacities, the means to proceed further. Indeed, for Aristotle, eggs are potential chickens but do possess an identity: their identity is as eggs, including the potential to develop into something else. The killing of a human fetus is thus no more murder than, say, the killing of a human tooth, appendix, or kidney (unless the death of those parts results in the death of the entire human being). That is to say, *being alive* is not sufficient to confer upon a cell or an organism the rights-bearing status of a human being.

There is much that is implied by all this, but what matters here is that any individual human being who lacks the capacity for generating at least rudimentary ideas (one manifestation of which is the ability to communicate by language) cannot be regarded as a "rational animal" in point of fact, even if there might be reason in a particular context to treat him as such. Of course, we are not talking about instances when one is asleep or under anesthesia. But if what seems to be a human individual is incapable of any manner of concept formation whatever, and simply lies around as a vegetable as his normal and unalterable state, then we may plausibly raise the issue of whether the person thus debilitated is actually a human being proper at all or merely appears to be so upon first inspection.

Of course, these issues are widely debated and new light might be shed upon them at any time. It is the kind of issue we run across at the edges of typical instances of some kind of thing. These are "borderline cases."

No one would think of allowing the killing of a ten-year-old child, nor would anyone debate (this side of a concentration camp) whether a healthy forty-year-old adult should be used for organ donation against her will. We may, however, legitimately debate whether a ten-week-old fetus might be killed, just as we may legitimately debate whether a brain-dead adult might be used as an organ donor or whether it is okay to help a terminally ill and suffering patient commit suicide. The unusual and borderline cases cannot be handled with the kind of confidence afforded typical cases, but it is by reference to the context established by the normal case that we can first determine what even constitutes a borderline case and, second, what sorts of principles we must deploy to grapple with such borderline cases.

As best as we can tell so far, the distinctively human capacity to reason does not emerge until the twenty-fourth week of pregnancy. Thus, for purposes of law, the pro-choice position should prevail until the twenty-fourth week of pregnancy and the pro-life position thereafter.

REFERENCES

Aquinas, Thomas. ca. 1476. *De Potentia Dei.* Cologne, Germany: Johann Koelhoff the Elder.

Feinberg, Joel. 1980. "Abortion." Pp. 183–217 in *Matters of Life and Death,* ed. Tom Regan. New York: Random House.

Ford, Norman M. 1989. *When Did I Begin? Conception of the Human Individual in History, Philosophy and Science.* Cambridge: Cambridge University Press.

Johnson, Gregory R., and David Rasmussen. 2000. "Rand on Abortion: A Critique." *The Journal of Ayn Rand Studies* 1, no. 2 (spring): 245–61.

Sturtevant, F. M. 1994. "Letter to the Editor." *The Wall Street Journal* (November 14), A11.

Wallace, William A. 1995. "St. Thomas on the Beginning and Ending of Human Life." Pp. 394–407 in *Sanctus Thomas de Aquino Doctor Hodiernae Humanitatis, Studi Tomistici* 58, ed. Autori Vari. Vatican City: Libreria Editrice Vaticana. Reprinted at www.nd.edu/Departments/Maritain/ti/wallace3.htm.

16

THE DESTRUCTIVE IRONIES
OF AFFIRMATIVE ACTION

Although the state's attempt to mandate what we now call affirmative action is fairly recent, the practice itself has existed a long time.

People have always chosen, on their own, to benefit members of some special group deemed to be disadvantaged in the context of commerce. Whenever a person patronizes a shop owned by someone from an actually or apparently disadvantaged group or hires someone from one of those groups, she is voluntarily doing the kind of thing that affirmative action policies attempt to impose by law. Similarly, patronizing a restaurant because one believes the owner needs some extra support so as to gain a foothold in the business is also an instance of affirmative action. Even buying works of art to encourage particular artists would count as affirmative action.

Thus, affirmative action is a familiar practice in life, albeit not so designated until recent times. Some black Americans acknowledge this, as did the late journalist Carl Rowan on C-SPAN a while back. He told a group of students that a white newspaper publisher had "practiced affirmative action" when he hired Rowan for his first job as a reporter. The boss apparently decided to give Rowan a chance because he was black: He wanted blacks to gain greater access to journalism. Obviously, the decision paid off for the employer as well, given Rowan's excellent performance on the job. And in justice, a prospective employee's qualifications for the job should surely be the dominant factor in any hiring decision. Certainly, one hopes that the attitude of Rowan's prospective employer was not, "Well, he'll be no good to the paper, but it would be nice to hire a black man"!

Such considerations point up the fact that even when entirely voluntary, a policy of positive discrimination is justified only as an exceptional or marginal matter: to help new arrivals in a country, for example; or, more generally, to help anyone suffering difficult straits who needs a temporary break. In such cases, affirmative action is more a matter of charity and good will than of attempting to expiate or redress an alleged collective guilt. But a private company's "affirmative action" is open to legitimate criticism if the policy is persistent, discriminates unjustly, and undermines good business.

Publicly held corporations, furthermore, could practice affirmative action only when those who own its stock have instructed management to do so. Affirmative action, rightly understood, is morally proper only when the specific, local details of a situation warrant it. Under ordinary circumstances, most publicly held companies would have little cause to practice it.

The brand of affirmative action debated today is, of course, that imposed by government policy. The state mandates that students or contractors be chosen on the basis of racial or sexual criteria irrelevant for the purpose at hand but thought to be helpful to members of the targeted group. The government decides which persons are appropriate candidates for the mandatory boost, presumably basing its criteria on certain sociological and historical facts pertaining to the disadvantages many members of the group in question have suffered in the past and the supposed benefits enjoyed as a consequence by the dominant groups, usually whites.

Those forced to "act affirmatively" are neither expected nor allowed to exercise discretion in the matter. Of course, some might well have done the "right thing" anyway, just as some volunteer to join the army during time of war whether or not conscription is in force. Except insofar as one has exercised a minor say-so through the democratic process, however, any credit or blame for the deed is voided by the bureaucrats. Many of those implementing affirmative action policies simply do what they're ordered to do, leaving it unknown and unknowable whether they followed their conscience or merely obeyed the point of a gun. That is what is meant by demoralization!

Mandatory affirmative action runs contrary to the goals and principles of properly and constitutionally limited government. Government confined to its proper scope of authority is obligated to serve well all those under its jurisdiction. That is the spirit underlying the Fourteenth Amendment to the U.S. Constitution: We ought all to be treated equally well under the law. That is what citizenship implies.[1] No one is to be specially privileged or specially burdened.

When governments engage in affirmative action, this principle is violated. That is one reason why the California affirmative action ban enacted by Proposition 209 makes good sense. Indeed, it should never have been necessary to hold a referendum about it in the first place. Governmentally imposed affirmative action is unjust. To be just, governments must relate to people as citizens, period, not as members of some specially privileged group in whom a special interest is taken at the expense of the rights of the rest of the citizenry.

Some will argue that government must indeed provide special protection to special groups, when their members are the target of injustice. Blacks, therefore, may receive special treatment because they are targets of unjust discrimination, something that affirmative action would redress. But this line of thinking presupposes the truth of a collectivist view of the world. In such a framework whites have treated blacks unjustly as a group, as have Germans treated Jews unjustly, capitalists treated workers unjustly, or Turks have treated Hungarians unjustly.

In the real world, however, particular individuals treat others justly or unjustly or are thus treated themselves. Injustice is never a matter of how groups behave or are being treated but only of how their members behave or are being treated, even if the thinking behind the unjust treatment is itself collectivist—for example, that all blacks, Jews, or Hungarians are unworthy or inferior.

Groups of human beings as such do not act; they are not independent, choosing organisms. The acting agent is the human individual. Any redress must, therefore, be a matter of rectifying or punishing the actions of those who actually committed the injustice. The rectification or punishment would be unjust if it were directed at all people who happen to belong to groups the *other* members of which have been unjust to some persons.

Under the logic of the collectivist, all of us would be rendered culpable on a great many questions besides that of racial discrimination. After all, any wrongdoer is a member of many groups. On collectivist grounds, all other members of those same groups—tall people, redheads, females, recipients of Social Security, immigrants, voters for Al Gore, or what have you—could be arbitrarily assigned culpability for the immoral acts—or given credit for the moral acts—perpetrated by some individuals who belong to them.

Consider the practice in Ghana where in many instances a young virgin from a family is given to a priest in order to atone for the sins of some elder of that family! Once the premise is granted that group identity is all that counts for purposes of redress and not individual moral responsibility, there is nothing in logic to prevent such a wholesale application of said principle. However, it is the height of injustice to punish the innocent just because they are involuntary members of a group in which some are guilty yet are no longer around to answer for what they've done. Visiting the punishment upon the offspring of the guilty is itself a guilty deed.

Governmentally dictated affirmative action based on such collectivist assignation of guilt is not only unjust: It can also be the source of serious resentment to anyone, racist or not.

Now, an individual's sovereignty—his freedom, for example, to associate only with those with whom he is willing to associate—should not be usurped by government, even if his judgment and conduct leave a lot to be desired. I may choose rotten pals, an unsuitable mate, or the wrong employee, but it is my life and what I do with it is properly up to me (as long as I don't choose to violate the same right of others), not those who would impose their judgment against my will.[2]

In any case, freedom of association is a hallmark of the free society—freedom of association across the board, even in cases in which such association is infected by irrational racism, ethnocentrism, sexism, or other kinds of unjustified prejudice. This is so even in cases in which those excluded forgo serious benefits as a result.

When associating with others, one is making a decision as to how one will live one's own life. To make a person devote her life or any portion of it to a purpose she rejects (and never contractually agreed to) amounts to subjecting the person to involuntary servitude, period. No free society can tolerate this, even for purposes that can be quite admirable.[3]

Law professor Richard Epstein, of the University of Chicago, has argued the radical but sound thesis that not even most of the civil rights legislation of the 1960s can be considered of real help to blacks and women in our society.[4] Epstein agrees that such legislation violates freedom of association by forcing people to hire and promote folks they may not want to. By this means, if not the letter then certainly the spirit of the American constitutional system is assaulted. Whatever gains may have been reaped through such legal action are marred by the fundamental flaw embodied in them.

Indeed, all civil rights legislation is wrong that goes beyond striking down racist and sexist policies by government, which would violate the Fourteenth Amendment's prohibition against denying to "to any person . . . equal protection of the laws." Mandatory affirmative action programs are also an insult to the people they are supposed to help. Certainly blacks and women have suffered a great variety of more or less severe injustice, as have members of other groups throughout human history, but mandated affirmative action treats intended beneficiaries as a group as if they were all incompetent to function as a result of that injustice upon some of them (or perhaps upon their parents or grandparents).

Are blacks and women really unable to rise from the ruins of their families? Well, innumerable Jews, Hungarians, Poles, and members of other groups throughout history have had to recover from terrific blows without the benefit of the U.S. Congress having legislated allegedly remedial public policy in the way of mandated affirmative action. Arguably, such coercive pampering can end up itself hampering recovery from setbacks by instilling in folks the conviction that they are, after all, not quite up to handling problems the way other people can.[5] It can be a psychic albatross.

A legally enforced policy of affirmative action may even exacerbate the irrationality and injustice it is intended to remedy. When citizens are regimented with respect to whom they hire or do business with, their judgment is coercively eclipsed and they are justified in resenting that. Indeed, such policies can actively encourage prejudice to linger even while driving it underground, for what folks will focus upon is not their own prejudicial conduct—which they might have been prompted to confront head-on had they been treated as morally sovereign agents capable of determining their own behavior. Instead they will focus upon having had their sovereignty denied, their freedom taken away. In that respect, they will have a legitimate complaint.

Affirmative action thus gives the racists among us a phony yet insidious new rationalization for racism—since now their animosity toward a minority has some semblance of justification: If women and blacks support mandated affirmative action, then there really is something wrong with women and blacks, isn't there? After all, they give backing to tyrannical policies of government! Just as blacks have had some justification for being suspicious of all whites when slavery and segregation were given support by most whites and not firmly enough rejected by the rest, so whites and members of other groups can develop similar attitudes when affirmative action is mandated that discriminates against them.

The irony is that mandated affirmative action may not really help those blacks and women who can use the help. Instead it is the middle-class blacks, the very people who can routinely make it on their own and have every chance to do so, who appear to get the extra, unfair boost. Those in really bad straits are often not even touched by this facade of assistance. But, although arguably nothing much of substance gets done for most blacks by affirmative action, the policy does everything to boost the self-image of racist Americans for now they can cloak their racism in a valid grievance. They can now hate the government for imposing plainly unfair, even racist policies. Sensing this psychology, those who support affirmative action will themselves sometimes feel justified in painting all critics of affirmative action as racists. What a mess!

In the social realm, it seems that progress in race relations has indeed been made, but that progress has been dampened and sometimes derailed by all the reliance on government remedies. These days, for example, being racist isn't acceptable in the Deep South. A while back, a hospital worker in Opelika, Alabama, made a racist remark to me about a black colleague. When I rebuked him for it, he said, "I am sorry; I am a racist but I cannot help it." This certainly showed not the usual self-righteous racism but only a desperate and feeble attempt at rationalization, suggesting that the man knew very well that his racism isn't something acceptable in a decent human being. Yet, if this guy were to lose a promotion to a black person because of mandated affirmative action, he would doubtless feel comfortable about hating blacks under the guise of hating big government. How convenient to not have to face openly your own most vile, irrational feelings!

If there is anyone who has very good reason for opposing affirmative action mandates by the government, it is American blacks. It is, as Shelby Steele noted on PBS's *News Hour*, a way for white liberals to feel good about themselves without actually having to do much of substance for anyone.[6]

17

THE BILL OF RIGHTS
AND MORAL PHILOSOPHY

E very person has the unalienable right to, among other
things, life, liberty, and the pursuit of happiness. This idea
certainly ignites the passion of anyone who appreciates how vital individual liberty is to human community life. Nowhere on
earth has the idea been more seriously considered as an element
of official political philosophy than in the United States. It has
inspired men and women throughout the globe for several centuries and continues to do so, especially if we are talking about
ordinary folks who aspire to emigrate to relatively free societies,
even from ones that aren't out-and-out tyrannies.

The United States' founders and framers had articulated
the principles of individual rights, both in the Declaration of
Independence and then, admittedly incompletely and tragically
compromised, in the U.S. Constitution's Bill of Rights. They
singled out certain rights or protections as deserving of special
mention without, however, belittling others not explicitly listed.

The central theme of these documents is the doctrine of
individual rights. Spelled out in considerable detail by the English philosopher John Locke, the doctrine acknowledges and
upholds the sovereignty of each human being, his right and capacity to choose his own path in life without arbitrary interference from others. If a person is sovereign, he is not to be fundamentally ruled by others or to rule *over* others. Rather, each
individual is taken to be properly in charge of his property and
person.

The founders of this country thereby rejected what was the most pervasive doctrine on the globe at the time: namely, that some people are justified—by God, nature, force, or convenience—to act as lords and masters over other people. The founders were not in full agreement about how thoroughly these ancient views should be rejected—thus the lifelong debate between Thomas Jefferson and Alexander Hamilton (and, most significantly, U.S. Supreme Court Chief Justice John Marshall).

By permitting slavery in the country governed by the Constitution, the framers were guilty of a tragic inconsistency. For nearly a century, the Constitution remained a contradictory document, and the contradiction took a civil war to rectify (and at once, also, to distort)—a conflict that in turn arguably generated another set of violations of sovereignty, the consequences of which we are still grappling with today. Still, it is worth noting that the abolitionists who helped rid the country of slavery found inspiration in the thought of those same founders. Without the philosophical base stated in the Declaration, it is doubtful that our country's heritage could have offered a solid political argument against slavery, an institution that was certainly not unique to the New World.

How does the doctrine of individual rights fare today among political philosophers? Not too well: In our time, few political philosophers champion this outlook. In other disciplines of the liberal arts, even fewer scholars—steeped as they are in relativism, determinism, and amoralism—have any respect for individual rights. Although lip service is still given to human rights (for example, by such "human rights watch" agencies as Amnesty International), the precise meaning of such rights has become all but totally obscure. In the past, the right to liberty meant that one was free to go about on one's own initiative without uninvited intrusion from others—and that it was impermissible to conscript others for the sake of even allegedly benign purposes. Today, "rights" have devolved into almost any kind of stipulated claim and are as prolific as tissue paper. One is said to have "rights" to nearly everything one might like;

hence the sundry entitlement programs that have nearly bankrupted this country.

Yet it isn't just that the alleged meaning of human rights has undergone a radical shift in meaning via splicing of the Lockean doctrine with utterly alien outlooks. Many political philosophers scoff at the idea of individual rights altogether. Having accepted the notion that truth is historically relative—in other words, that we know what we know only as determined by our particular, historically determined viewpoint, one that enjoys no universal validity—these scribblers dismiss the notion of individual sovereignty as a mere relic of the past, a mere artifact of eighteenth-century mythology.

Meanwhile, other theorists (who also adopt the relativistic viewpoint when it suits them) don't hesitate to indict "us" for our past treatment of Native Americans, blacks, women, and other groups. Here, suddenly, universally objective moral standards have weight, and it is appropriate to blame our forefathers for their bigotry and sexism. The paradox is that even the out-and-out relativists take such indictments seriously, even though the indictments apply contemporary value judgments to historical periods not our own. This double standard is one of the great mysteries of contemporary political discussion. An uncharitable observer might chalk it up to hypocrisy.

Spelling out the ethical and political ideas embodied in the Bill of Rights will help us see just how unjustified historicist skepticism is with respect to that wonderful document. Not that everyone at the time of the writing of the Declaration and the Constitution understood the case for the various provisions exactly as I will spell it out here. Rather, my aim is only to show what can be said in support of the provisions of these documents without distorting their original sense and to suggest the universal validity of the principles implicitly defended.

The First Amendment lays out that Congress shall make no law prohibiting or abridging the crucial human activities of speech, press, assembly, or the petitioning of the government for a redress of grievances. How does this prohibition square with moral sense? Well, morality requires that (1) each person be free to make choices about what she will do and (2) there be identifiable standards by which to determine whether our choices are better or worse. By forbidding the federal government from dictating our thinking or its expression, the First Amendment pays direct attention to the moral nature of our lives by placing a firm border, which others may not cross, around each person's right to think, worship, and speak as she judges best.

The Second Amendment evinces firm respect for every person's life and liberty by making it clear that no one is to be deprived of the capacity to defend himself against aggressors. The right to bear arms is the right of self-defense, a right that flows from the basic value of life for each individual. Again, the amendment expresses no mere artifact of eighteenth-century preferences but a fundamental principle that is valid and relevant in any era in which a person might possibly be assaulted—in other words, any era.

The Third Amendment protects an aspect of the right to private property by prohibiting government's use of private homes in time of peace. It is clear from this amendment that the right to private property—a right that affirms in practical terms the basic right to life and liberty—was a vital aspect of the politics of the framers. They realized that the exercise of liberty requires a sphere of personal jurisdiction that is secured via property law.

The Fourth Amendment, which protects us against unreasonable searches and seizures, extends the idea of private property rights to cases in which there can be understandable temptation to violate them. Even when there is an emergency or state of siege, there may only be *reasonable* search and seizure: Only with good reason to back it up may the government intrude upon the privacy of its citizens.

This makes moral sense. When a crime is committed, citizens of a free society are obliged to support efforts to rectify matters. Without reasonable search and seizure powers, such rectification is impossible; how else could the government's detectives conduct a process of discovery and arrest a suspect? But the government cannot act willy-nilly whenever it has a hunch or impulse. Standards of reasonableness must guide the process. Such standards cannot of course be laid out with total precision for all situations, without regard to context, but they must exist and they must be clear, objective, and based on evidence. Here is a clear case of a procedural right that derives from the more fundamental right to life and liberty.

The Fifth Amendment also illustrates the moral awareness of our framers. It provides that except for military legal procedures—in which the task is necessarily guided by emergency conditions—the government must lay out a detailed indictment citing reasonable grounds for suspicion in order to restrain someone. Given that such a process is adhered to, it makes sense that in a free society devoted to maintaining justice, cooperation with the legal workings of government is mandated. This, incidentally, justifies the subpoena process as well. If individual citizens are to enjoy the fruits of a just society, they may not exempt themselves from participating when the wheels of justice uniquely require their presence. Self-incrimination, in turn, may not be coerced, since that would be to treat an accused person as if he or she had already been proved guilty and could be forced to behave in various punitive, untoward ways.

The Fifth Amendment further provides that no person may be deprived of any right without due process of law: the presentation of evidence, in an orderly legal procedure, justifying reasonable suspicion, probable cause, clear and present danger, and the like. Barring these necessary conditions, no action may be taken that impinges on the normal rights of citizens. Finally, the amendment stipulates that now and then private property may have to be used for public purposes. This, again, makes sense: Courthouses, police stations, military bases, and the like need to be built. These bona fide "public" concerns are not to be confused with the bloated rendition of "public" employed in our times, however, whereby anything any sizable number of the citizenry happen to desire becomes a public purpose. Only when these proper public uses are at issue may government engage in takings, and only if the market price is paid for what is taken. To be sure, in most or all cases the requisite property could simply be acquired voluntarily, just as property is bought and sold every day in the marketplace for private purposes. Ideally, the government should take property over by force only in a rare emergency, a condition one could spell out explicitly.

The Sixth Amendment speaks of a "right to a speedy and public trial," thus specifying further certain procedural implications for a legal system grounded in justice, in a genuinely free society in which citizens are recognized as sovereign. The same observation applies to the Seventh and Eighth Amendments, which uphold the right of trial by jury and ban "cruel and unusual" punishment.

The unfortunately neglected Ninth Amendment unequivocally affirms—despite all the feigned doubt expressed about it—the fact that citizens have other, implicit rights, depending on their various circumstances, that are derived from the rights affirmed both in the Declaration of Independence and in the amendments cited earlier. Since the Constitution is a brief and concise document, it cannot be expected to enter the details of the theory of rights guiding it, so the framers make clear in the Ninth Amendment that they have not forgotten the broader framework guiding their political and legal deliberations. This amendment also imposes an obligation on legislators and courts to discover and protect any further rights legitimately held by the people. In short, the Ninth Amendment is a code of professional ethics for our political representatives and appointed officials. It is, of course, often utterly ignored.

The Tenth Amendment—stipulating that powers not delegated to the federal government by the Constitution or prohibited by it to the states are reserved to the states or to the people—may be understood as exemplifying a contextualist approach to the law. Concerning many issues, the federal government could not be expected to have much expertise and therefore should not meddle in them. It is, indeed, prohibited from doing so—it is beyond its range of authority, its jurisdiction. The law, after all, must be implemented locally, attending to the facts of life specific to the region. Some of these facts will apply generally enough and thus may be treated by the federal government; others have no relevance outside of the local context. Thus we have different governmental bodies—from the federal down to the municipal levels. None of these laws may violate the individual rights of the citizenry. Apart from that prohibition, however, the different governmental bodies will have needs for different powers and jurisdictions.

There is a lot more to morality than what the laws of a just legal system contain, but these laws certainly have moral content and foundation. Furthermore, they suggest moral considerations even beyond those entailed by their immediate explication: for example, the idea of individual responsibility for one's life and the virtues of prudence, courage, and honesty. After all, the affirmation of personal autonomy does not make sense unless human beings are capable of self-government and have the responsibility of self-government.

The statement of the Declaration of Independence that "all men are created equal and are endowed by their creator with certain unalienable rights, among them life, liberty, and the pursuit of happiness" amounts to a philosophical preamble to our system of justice. Among its other laudable features, the statement is unique and praiseworthy for its affirmation of our right to pursue happiness. In previous eras such a pursuit was generally deemed to be negligible, even unworthy. Except for a few rare philosophers, most thinkers through the ages have regarded human beings as obliged to pursue not their own personal happiness but service to God or to humanity.

Finally, with the founding of the United States, the validity of the pursuit of happiness was not only acknowledged but was also enshrined—hailed as an inalienable right—in the very founding documents of the country. Intellectuals have responded either by declaring this emphasis to be mistaken altogether or by proposing that it is not the right to *pursue* happiness that should be stipulated and safeguarded, but the "right" to *achieve* it (have it handed to one on a silver platter). Right-wingers tend to take the former line, left-wingers the latter.

The founders had it dead right. The freedom to pursue happiness is of the utmost importance, and that is all that a community can practically do to help bring about an individual's personal happiness: Remove unnecessary impediments to the seeking. Happiness cannot be legally mandated or handed out in Cracker Jacks boxes. It is an internally generated condition. And *this* is a universal fact of life, true in any age. In this respect, as in most others, the founding fathers saw that the libertarian polity is indeed not only most useful but also most just.

Will we live up to their legacy? Unfortunately, the substance of that legacy has been increasingly challenged and undercut with the passage of time, particularly in the halls of academe. Fortunately, those who inhabit those halls are not quite the godlike shapers of the course of history they sometimes like to think they are. As long as our right to free thought is still respected in at least the law, we the people are still in charge. We can still decide between a future guided by the principles that gave birth to our nation—or alien and destructive ones that will send us lurching back into a dark age of feudalism and arbitrary rule.

One can only hope. As the founders knew, we are free to choose.

18

THE MEDIA VERSUS FREEDOM: SOME CASES IN POINT

It's a wonder that the citizens of the United States are able to enjoy any freedom at all, given how poorly freedom fares in the eyes of media mavens charged with teaching us every day what is going on and why. Everything from mergers to junk mail seems to chronically get the back of their hand. Only when the media itself is threatened with government meddling do journalists speak in defense of liberty—their own, that is!

The same is the case with academe. Any threat of academic freedom, other than in the name of political correctness, is met with resistance from the community of scholars and teachers, but the call from their ranks for more and more government regulation of the economy is notorious.

WELLS FARGO AND THE PRESS

When, in late January 1996, California's Wells Fargo Bank acquired First Interstate Bank in what the press so gleefully likes to call a hostile takeover, I was in California, driving from one place to another for various speaking engagements. So I had the opportunity to listen to innumerable news reports discussing the purchase—particularly the fare on KCBS-AM radio, the all-news station in San Francisco.

Invariably, the broadcasters stressed one particular aspect of this major economic event: the likelihood that thousands of First Interstate employees would lose their jobs in Wells Fargo's efforts to consolidate its services and to secure a more profitable operation for the resulting huge enterprise. Distraught employees were interviewed. Journalists pretending to have some measure of economic and business expertise gave their views on the matter. Invariably, the main message relayed was how this major buyout would hurt people—even consumers (seeing as how the reduction in the workforce surely couldn't be good for customers).

Not one person advanced the idea that such a merger would probably enrich many Wells Fargo and First Interstate stockholders, or that these people would now be able to invest more money into their children's education, health care, clothing, ballet lessons, and other efforts to make a better life for themselves. Nor, again, was it noted—not even by the alleged economists—that the merger would very likely lead to *more* demand for labor, giving those who leave the employ of First Interstate Bank another opportunity for productive employment. Nobody mentioned that if economic stasis were in fact preferable to economic growth that happens to disrupt the lives of some in the short term, then it was a blunder even to emerge from the Stone Age—and we should certainly never have replaced the candle with the lightbulb, or the horse and buggy with the automobile.

That this particular merger would have a long-run salutary impact was not certain, of course—but neither was it certain that those laid off from the merger could find no work, even better work, through which to earn a living. Yet the media experts immediately zeroed in on the possible downsides, skipping over any possible positives. The one mention of benefit—the possible profitability of the merger—came as a snide remark, making clear that the experts regarded the hope for profit to be a crass motive indeed for doing such terrible things as consolidating two giant financial institutions. Once again, the pursuit of prosperity was relegated to the status of a cancerous virus that merely hurts people. Yet it is precisely the realization of greater profitability that would demonstrate that the merger was indeed a good idea vis-à-vis its general economic impact over the long haul. An economist might have deigned to point that out.

With rare exceptions like *The Wall Street Journal*, *Investment Business Daily*, *Forbes*, and *Barron's*, such narrow-mindedness about affairs of business seems to afflict nearly all news reporting. If there were such a thing as a tradition of class-action malpractice suits against the press, one could make a very strong case against all the reporters whose only aim seems to be to disparage business and scare the hell out of the public.

What can be done about this? Well, it would be nice if business schools and other educational institutions made some effort to teach journalism majors some measure of economic wisdom. That would not be enough, though, for economists typically try to avoid giving a moral defense of the market. What is really necessary is *moral* education of the public— including the press—about how prosperity is a decent objective and that those who pursue it are doing the right thing. It's unlikely, however, our educational system will routinely deliver this kind of moral lesson anytime soon.

PAYING MANAGEMENT WHILE DOWNSIZING

It is lucky for the employees of the CBS television magazine program *60 Minutes* that the First Amendment to the U.S. Constitution does not permit the government to license and regulate reporters. If any kind of standards for economic literacy had to be followed by reporter Leslie Stahl, for example—so that when she discusses matters of commerce, her listeners could be reasonably sure that she would ask intelligent questions—she'd be out on her ear.

In a recent segment in which she interviewed executives and other professionals laid off by firms struggling to trim their operations, Stahl demonstrated both her sentimentality and her journalistic malpractice. One of the interviewees expressed outrage at the fact that he was laid off even as higher management got raises, yet Stahl never bothered to suggest that perhaps one reason for this is that higher management made very good decisions in pursuing the policy of downsizing—that they were, perhaps, therefore more valuable to the company. It is a task of good management to learn how to make a company profitable. This is a manager's professional responsibility; this is why she is hired. Making the tough calls is part of the job.

In all fields of employment, there are times when downsizing is advisable. If, on such occasions, a firm fails to trim costs, it fails those who depend upon it with their investment. Football teams, orchestras, faculties at universities, hospitals, television broadcasters, and every other kind of employer find that without restructuring and cost-cutting, they will have no future at all, let alone a downsized one.

60 Minutes itself could experience some downsizing. If it were to fall in the ratings, some changes would have to be made. Perhaps it would have to be scrapped entirely. Leslie Stahl is too much of a star, of course, to be in danger of a major career setback, but it is not out of the question. So if not for the sake of her viewers, then at least for her own sake she should familiarize herself with the realities of the business world. One is that a firm does not exist primarily for the sake of making its loyal employees happy, secure, and satisfied. It exists to further the goals of those who own it, so that they can send their kids to college, take vacations, pay the mortgage, and eat healthy meals. Employees should therefore never become complacent. Rather, they should look for ever more ways to make themselves invaluable to those who hire them.

Such observations of course upset many cultural commentators. They imagine that some other economic system would do better. But that is a myth: There are no risk-free economic systems. In a capitalist system, though, one is at least never deceived about security. So one can buy insurance, set aside resources for times of economic hardship, improve one's skills, and otherwise prepare for the twists and turns of fate. By contrast, socialist systems sell their citizens a bill of goods; then, when the roof caves in, everyone screams his disappointment when the illusion of security proves in fact to be illusory.

In the United States, too, there is now too much complacency about security. People are being told that the world owes them a living, that they have "a right to a job," "a right to health care and social security," and so forth. No wonder, then, that the laid-off executives and professionals are baffled, their self-esteem damaged, their souls curdled. They've bought into the notion that when the market can no longer sustain them in their preferred line of work, they are being cheated. They do not consider that customers may have changed their buying habits, which is often exactly what is happening.

Perhaps it is too much to expect economic and moral literacy from every working stiff, but it would be nice if a star reporter at the nation's most prestigious television news magazine did consider such matters and maybe even broached them as appropriate while on the job—so that she could do that job well and properly.

THE WELFARE STATE AND THE NEWS

I have a hypothesis. I would like readers to test it. My hypothesis is that in the welfare state, news reporting has been taken over by lobbying that masquerades as news.

Not counting stories about peace agreements or who won the Nobel Prize, nearly every news item these days seems to feature some event or situation in which people want something and the government is being called upon to provide it. It has become par for the course for reporters on *20/20* or *60 Minutes* to indignantly exclaim that although a certain problem exists, "the government has done nothing about it." Not only reporters but producers, too, appear to be focusing on stories that in their view evoke the need for some kind of government action. Indeed, it is a feather in the cap of a news organization if a story it has produced inspires some politician to introduce a bill, call a hearing, or promise some kind of reform. If the story pertains to the demands of some sizable group in our society, journalistic "success" is nearly assured. Pulitzer Prizes, for example, tend to be doled out to those whose "news" constitutes a "public service," not exactly a criterion grounded in journalistic standards per se.

Clearly, in a welfare state the prospects for such "news" casting are fabulous. Given the incentives, why should reporters, commentators, producers, and the like ever consider that it could be in the public interest to shut the doors of government to all such demands? To do that would be to bar a large percentage of their stories from ever "making a difference." They might even have to consider pursuing some genuine news. Even, heaven forfend, *good* news.

As long as the welfare state is the status quo, we can count on floods of such stories day after day, week after week, month after month, decade after decade. Except for a few outré rags with the axe of liberty to grind, few of those in charge will encourage truly critical scrutiny of mainstream political affairs. Few, if any, will raise such questions as: "Why should government deprive the successful of the fruits of their success, just because there are some who do not enjoy the same? What justification is there for demanding such pseudo–Robin Hoodism?" (It's pseudo because Robin Hood actually took back from those who taxed the poor what they took!) Or: "Mr. President, if we spend more money on your programs, our non-voting children will have to be taxed for this. So does this not violate the principle 'No taxation without representation'?" Or: "If, according to the criminal law, it is wrong to punish people unless they have been proved guilty of a crime, why is it that government regulations may impose enormous economic burdens on people who have done nothing wrong? Isn't this a kind of prior restraint that is disallowed in a free society?" Or: "If the Fourteenth Amendment prohibits the unequal application of the law, why is it that although producers are prohibited from discriminating, consumers can do so with total impunity? And why can government regulate every profession but the press, arts, and clergy—is this not a built-in inequality, a state-sponsored and systematic discrimination?"

But when the so-called news organizations feed off the welfare state so successfully, what motive do they have—not counting the trivial one of a desire to pursue the truth—to express even the most natural doubts about welfare statism as they hobnob with leaders of state on *Meet the Press, This Week, Face the Nation,* and all the rest?

It would take some genuine journalistic integrity to do so, integrity of the kind people seem to praise only when they observe it in reporters overseas as they risk life and limb to expose the deeds of some murderous tyrant. When no firing squad threatens, and nothing much but one's cushy livelihood as an alleged reporter is at stake, it seems that the courage to challenge the status quo may be forsaken with impunity.

That's my hypothesis, anyway. You can test it yourself the next time you pick up a newspaper or turn on the television.

JUNK MAIL AND BENEVOLENCE

On the Internet a while ago, I received a message that had been forwarded to me—paradoxically enough, about how awful junk mail is, whether it is paper or electronic. I read through the elaborate discussion, including lengthy advice on how one can combat this evil thing in our midst, and some of it did resonate with me a bit. After all, much of the email in my inbox is totally useless to me, and I must expend several seconds a day deleting it.

Yet a bit of reflection will reveal how misguided all this animosity toward junk mail—and, indeed, advertising in general—really is. Let's set aside the question of the subsidies given to advertisers by the U.S. Postal Service. There is no way to price services in a government-created, government-protected monopoly such as the postal service that truly reflects how a competitive, market-based firm would have done it. In an actual market, such subsidies (or discounts) might be justified by the scale of the traffic involved, or they might not. Only the results achieved by profit-seeking firms will tell the tale.

Setting that economic question aside, what about the moral status of sending out so-called junk mail? What about advertising in general?

Junk mail and other ads are the calls people issue to others to consider purchasing their products or services. Advertising makes it possible for many people to earn a living. Given all the bellyaching about downsizing and job security, it's odd to find fault with those who attempt to secure jobs and employment via a means that is decent, honest, and ultimately harmless. Advertising also supports an array of entertainment and news, come to think of it—which we don't have to pay for with anything other than a bit of patience.

Nonetheless, a good many pundits and politicians would rather have us enslaved to the workers, forced to pay them or to buy their products—as opposed to, say, buying the products and services of Europeans or Asians. In short, we shouldn't make choices about who we deal with but have this forced upon us by laws that require us to deal with certain parties. This kind of involuntary servitude seems to be the preferred solution—it is not so annoying as having to put up with calls from telemarketers or junk mailers.

Of course, there is the junk mail from nonprofit agencies—from people trying to collect funds for one or another good cause or to enable them to run for political office. Those who beef about this are, to my mind, certainly not entitled to consider themselves compassionate and kind.

It is, after all, pretty simple to delete junk e-mail or toss junk snail mail. Moreover, TVs have remote controls now, not to mention mute buttons. So maybe we can be gracious enough to tolerate the efforts of those trying to make a living through advertising that offers their wares, while admitting that now and then they commit infelicities in the process.

EPILOGUE

I chose *The Passion for Liberty* as my title in part because I know of books with titles such as *The Passion for Equality, The Passion for Fairness,* and *The Passion for Justice,* and it seemed that it's about time to have a book with the title and subject matter of this work. The very idea of passion has often been demeaned in connection with liberty or its philosophical champions, classical liberals. Ludwig von Mises tells us, for example:

> No sect and no political party has believed that it could afford to forgo advancing its cause by appealing to men's senses. Rhetorical bombast, music, and song resound, banners wave, flowers and colors serve as symbols, and the leaders seek to attach their followers to their own person. Liberalism has nothing to do with all this. It has no party flowers and no party color, no party song and no party ideals, no symbols and no slogans. It has the substance and the arguments. These must lead it to victory.[1]

Ironically, Mises has become one of the several idols of classical liberalism and rightly so, because in this respect he was wrong. There is nothing wrong with some pomp when it comes to the championing of great ideas, even ideas that have all the substance and argument in their favor.

In this work, I do not at all shy away from showing the merits of some of these ideas but I wanted, also, to put on record

209

a certain measure of enthusiasm and awe where the idea and prospects of liberty are concerned. There is nothing wrong, indeed everything right, with human beings feeling and showing passion in support of what is good and right and beautiful, and liberty is certainly all these and more once it is well understood.

There would be a certain vital lack in the case for liberty if it could not inspire a bit of excitement. Human beings are built in such a way as to become passionate for what they believe is right and good, so once the substance and the arguments have been laid out, it is time to become inspired and make that inspiration do its job of supporting the substance and arguments and hard work that must follow for the ideas and ideals of liberty to take practical hold.

In my life, I have tried to do my best to study the substance and arguments for all the major and some of the minor ideas and ideals proposed to guide us in our personal and social lives, but none has inspired me so much as those that back up the free society. This is what I meant to show in the work I placed before the reader here. The basic thrust of why I am convinced that everyone's right to liberty must be protected by the legal system of a just community is this:

Jean-Jacques Rousseau said that he wanted "the reign of virtue" throughout the world. My friendly contemporary adversary, Professor Jim Sterba of the University of Notre Dame, wrote a book titled *How to Make People Just,* and another well-known philosopher, Professor Robert George, wrote one with the title *Making Men Moral.* The point of Rousseau's, Sterba's, and George's idea is to force adult human beings, at least in some crucial situations—for example, when others need their good conduct—into being good, nothing less.

This dream has been at the center of much of moral philosophy, as well as much of political theory, although by all accounts it seems to be an impossible dream, maybe even a wicked one. The very idea of being morally good, of conducting oneself virtuously, rests on something that stands in the way of ever forcing or making people good. This is our free will, the capacity to initiate our actions. To be morally good requires that one *choose* to do what is right, not be made to do it. Being made to do something robs one of the chance of doing the right—or, for that matter, the wrong—thing. The behavior itself will lack moral significance if it is forced on someone.

Yet the fanciful desire for a managed good world is extremely strong. Many, therefore, are completely willing to evade this most elementary fact of human life, namely, that ethical conduct is impossible when someone is forced to behave in ways that would, if chosen, be morally virtuous.

The strong desire to have a morally perfect world, society, culture, or age has inspired thousands of philosophers, theologians, politicians, bureaucrats, reformers, revolutionaries, and the like to advocate deploying force so as to guarantee their utopia of a morally decent population. One strong reason is that so many other things in nature seem to be open to human control. Science and technology, including all the crafts and the engineering fields, happily take it that forcibly imposing order on the world is a good thing.

It is about time, however, to abandon the wish that people can be made good the way that plants in one's garden can be made to flourish. If there is anything truly unique about human beings, it is that their morally significant conduct, the kind that can be right or wrong and for which they may be praised or blamed, must be chosen.

People's lives depend, in large measure, on their making sound choices, taking the initiative, and doing things sensibly and wisely instead of expecting the impersonal forces of nature to guide them, as is the case with most other living beings, ones guided by their genetic makeup, instincts, or similar hardwiring.

One reason that we disagree with one another so much, why those who read these lines can raise questions and offer criticisms of what they are reading, is grounded in this freedom. Their choices can be different from mine. Being wrong, believing what is false, and, especially, neglecting to figure things out carefully are quintessential human capacities. Of course, these capacities also make possible incredible achievements, innovations, and originality in science, art, entertainment, and the whole array of human affairs.

All of this, however, comes with a price: None of it can be guaranteed. No formula exists to get us to do what is right or to be good people, contrary to all the dreams. The most we can do is discover some sensible rules and write them down and protect them as best we can, but this requires an inordinate degree of vigilance without any chance of guaranteed success. When Aristotle proposed that one of government's central tasks is to make people virtuous, he was talking mostly of small communities and may, in fact, have had in mind that virtuous conduct requires support from one's community, which is exactly right. But the kind of support that modern governments try to deploy, namely, the force of laws and regulations, is very ill suited for encouraging virtue and mostly demoralizes society instead.

The imposition of "the reign of virtue" is not just a flawed vision but also an out-and-out threat to the chance for bona fide virtue in human life, the kind of virtue that comes from the individual person who has chosen to do what is right.

As a final note in these reflections on liberty, I wish to deal with one way that many critics have approached ideas that champion principled public policy measures instead of piecemeal, pragmatic politics. It is to dismiss the view as mere ideology. What the view is, in fact, is principled political thinking, and there is no need to apologize for it unless it is just wrongheaded.

In this work as in others I have produced, I have followed a form of thinking pertaining to public policy that is often demeaned and shown rather surly and smug disdain by many detractors. They claim that such thinking is a relic of the past now. It may have had merit at the time of the American founders, but some find it utter folly to take this seriously in our time. (This was the point of my discussion in chapter 8.)

Those who deny the relevance of principled thinking to our political life argue that human life, including public affairs, is too variable, unsteady, chaotic, and irrational to yield to any systematic approach. The charge gains support not just from certain current trends, such as postmodernism, deconstructionism, and radical pragmatism, as well as the earlier idea of historicism, the notion that each epoch of human history requires a new order, but it also gets some support from the hectic nature of human life conveyed in the media—innumerable bits and pieces of human affairs seemingly unconnected by any measure of coherence.

The demeaning of principles also gains support from how little systematic thinking most citizens seem to engage in when they reflect about politics, let alone when they argue for various public policies. The influence of special or vested interests of one or another group such as farmers, merchants, educators, artists, and scientists—as well as of ethnic, racial, and sexual minorities—contributes to the appearance of the helter-skelter nature of human public life.

So, when it comes to public discussions of politics, different general systems of ideas come off not as honest arguments dealing with how best to understand human public life in general. Instead, they are made to appear as different forms of idiocy, as nonsense, by those who oppose them. But that isn't the way to deal with such ideas, whatever general system they support.

It is the task of liberal education to explore which of such ideas makes the best sense, and it does them all a disservice to simply dismiss certain ones as ideology (which means, to those who use it to dismiss ideas with which they disagree, mere rationalizations for class interests). Disciplines such as political philosophy, political science, sociology, cultural anthropology, and political economics all attempt to address the issue of whether human political life can be something systematic and principled or whether it must be accepted that politics is fragmented, chaotic, and incapable of being understood in terms of some general principles.

Oddly, though, even while the current trends favor the piecemeal, pragmatic way of thought, there is no hesitation on the part of many to demand of professionals, especially those in the world of business, to act with integrity, to be consistent and upright, and to be, in other words, principled agents in their field on whom the public can depend. Thus, it looks like in ethics or morality the postmodernist trends have not managed to infiltrate.

Whether the piecemeal, pragmatic approach or a more principled one ought to prevail cannot be decided in a brief last note. Suffice it to say that there is a respectable enough case for considering human political life systematically. The idea should not simply be dismissed as if those taking that approach suffered from some kind of affliction or mental impairment.

Even if the events of political life appear to be without clear rhyme or reason, quite possibly the founders and the revolutionaries were right: Some kind of coherent, principled view is closer to the truth about politics than is the piecemeal approach. Whether it is capitalism, socialism, the welfare state, or some other system that fits human community life better, and by which our lives will make the most sense and will be most prosperous and happy, is something that we need to attend to.

Of course, although the systematic approach looks quite indispensable for the establishment, maintenance, and protection of a decent political community, one that does justice to the political concerns of human life, the actual events of political life can be influenced by all sorts of circumstances outside of what people believe. Economic, technological, climatic, and ecological factors, not to mention the often thoughtless reactions of people to these, have a serious impact on politics. The point, however, is not that politics is uninfluenced by all sorts of factors, but only that citizens ought to work hard in a way that is guided, mainly, by principled thinking.

There are many social and political theorists who find fault with this. They tend to think that principled thinking introduces top-down management in political life and thus encourages dictatorship and central planning. They believe that deliberate fashioning of political institutions leads to the rule of some kind of elite with special skills and the feeling of self-importance regarding how political life should be.

But there is no reason to think that principled—or, loosely labeled, ideological—thinking by citizens in a society cannot also be a strong bulwark against corruption, including tyranny and various degrees of central, top-down, paternalistic planning. If citizens recognized, in a principled fashion, that it is wrong to thwart human liberty, to undermine the primary role of individual sovereignty, initiative, and spontaneity, in human community life, they can be on guard regarding whoever would offer up solutions to social problems without loyalty to this insight.

Indeed, the opposition is badly conceived to be between those who think that systematic thinking is good for politics versus those who believe that we should leave everything to some sort of natural evolution that human thinking must not disturb. Human thinking is the natural evolution that influences human social life and the only option before us is whether this thinking is going to be sound, logical, truthful, and diligent or, rather, sloppy, helter-skelter, reckless, impulsive, dishonest, and lazy. We would do well to recall Blaise Pascal, who implored us, "Let us labour, then, to think well, for such is the foundation of morality."[2]

It is, in any case, a serious distraction, propagated by many political players, to dismiss the systematic approach as mere ideology, as some kind of dogmatic, inflexible, unrealistic approach to governing a society. What is important is that citizens—upon whom the direction of societies ought to rest and on whom, especially in near-democratic systems, direction actually depends—not be misled by heated rhetoric into believing that politics cannot be discussed in a principled fashion. General ideas matter, even if those who do not like them refuse to debate them and instead dismiss them as mere ideology. Whenever that term enters the political arena, one can be sure that the real issues are crucial: what kind of country should we have, what system of laws ought we to live by.

Ideologies—rather sketchy conceptions of the systems by which a legal order operates—can be either sound or unsound. Despite what Marx preached, namely that an ideology is merely a disguise for vested interest, and what some others believe, namely that it is a shortcut to careful and in-depth thinking about human public life, a carefully conceived framework for public affairs is indispensable. To dismiss this is itself simplistic: It fails to appreciate the role of general, abstract ideas that political philosophers, theorists, and even principled ordinary citizens need to order their actions and give support to systematic approaches to guiding public life.

NOTES

INTRODUCTION

1. For a discussion of those stirrings in Aristotle, see Fred D. Miller, Jr., *Nature, Justice, and Rights: Aristotle's Politics* (Oxford: Clarendon Press, 1995). See also Brian Tierney, "Origins of Natural Rights Language: Texts and Contents, 1150–1250," *History of Political Thought* 10 (1989): 615–46; and Cary J. Nederman, "Property and Protest: Political Theory and Subjective Rights in Fourteenth-Century England," *The Review of Politics* 58 (spring 1996): 323–44. These studies confirm the utter wrongheadedness of both Straussean and neo-Marxian notions—articulated in the works of Leo Strauss, C. B. Macpherson, and Alasdair MacIntyre—to the effect that no conception of individuality or of political individualism can be found prior to the sixteenth century.

2. There were many ideas that influenced the American founding, but those that were distinct had to do with positioning the individual citizen as the centerpiece of political value.

3. This kind of corruption of sound ideas is common—it's the result of both confusion and ill will. Consider how readily the idea of democracy fell prey to misapplication at the hands of the Marxists. They meant by it not the participation of all in political decision making but the rule of the party for what Marxist theory prescribed as the true goal of the people. Also, some have gotten impatient about rights because of how others have corrupted the idea, but that's not the right remedy. See Tibor R. Machan, "Wronging Rights," *Policy Review*, no. 17 (1981): 37–58.

4. Of course, that isn't to say that the freest country has been fully free—its history shows innumerable departures from that practically possible but difficult to attain ideal.

5. I note this because it is contested in contemporary philosophy by many prominent thinkers (e.g., the late Willard van Orman Quine at Harvard University).

6. Tibor R. Machan, "Epistemology and Moral Knowledge," *The Review of Metaphysics* 36 (September 1982): 23–49; and Tibor R. Machan, *Individuals and Their Rights* (La Salle, Ill.: Open Court Publishing Co., 1989), chapter 1.

7. For a distinction between personal and political norms, see Douglas B. Rasmussen and Douglas J. Den Uyl, *Liberty and Nature: An Aristotelian Defense of Liberal Order* (LaSalle, Ill.: Open Court Publishing Co., 1991).

8. For more on naturalism, see Tibor R. Machan, *Human Rights and Human Liberties* (Chicago: Nelson-Hall, 1975); and Douglas Rasmussen, "Essentialism, Values and Rights," in T. R. Machan, ed., *The Libertarian Reader* (Totowa, N.J.: Rowman & Littlefield, 1982), 37–52.

9. Tibor R. Machan, "A Reconsideration of Natural Rights Theory," *American Philosophical Quarterly* 19 (January 1982): 61–72; Tibor R. Machan, "Toward a Theory of Natural Individual Human Rights," *The New Scholasticism* 61 (winter 1987): 33–78; and Machan, *Individuals and Their Rights*.

10. Some dispute that it is only human beings who have basic rights to life, liberty, and property. Tom Regan has argued this on grounds, in part, that animals, too, have the capacity to think. See, for example, Tom Regan, *The Case for Animal Rights* (Berkeley: University of California Press, 1984). Cf. my "Do Animals Have Rights?" *Public Affairs Quarterly* 5 (April 1991): 163–73.

11. John Locke, *Second Treatise of Civil Government* (Chicago: Henry Regnery Company, 1955), 5.

12. For Immanuel Kant, both a modern defender of bona fide ethics and a political liberal, this freedom could be secured only via the "noumenal" realm of being (as opposed to the "phenomenal" realm available to our senses) since it could not be reconciled with the prevailing philosophy of physics of the time. In our day, however, natural science does not stand in the way of free will. See Roger W. Sperry, "Changing Concepts of Consciousness and Free Will," *Perspectives in Biology and Medicine* 9 (Autumn 1976): 9–19.

13. Machan, *Individuals and Their Rights.* The choice in question may perhaps be characterized better by calling it an act of initiation (of thought).

14. I am here drawing on Ayn Rand, "The Objectivist Ethics," *The Virtue of Selfishness: A New Concept of Egoism* (New York: Signet Books, 1964). See, for more, my "Reason, Individualism, and Capitalism: The Moral Vision of Ayn Rand," in D. Den Uyl and D. Rasmussen, eds., *The Philosophic Thought of Ayn Rand* (Urbana: University of Illinois Press, 1983).

15. Plato's conception of justice is broader than the justice that can characterize a political community. See Hannah F. Pitkin, *Wittgenstein and Justice* (Berkeley: University of California Press, 1972), 303ff.

16. I develop in detail the argument for the obligatory nature of these rights for human individuals in the context of their community lives, in Machan, *Individuals and Their Rights,* chapter 7.

17. John Rawls, *A Theory of Justice* (Cambridge, Mass.: Harvard University Press, 1971), 104: "The assertion that a man deserves the superior character that enables him to make the effort to cultivate his abilities is . . . problematic; for his character depends in large part upon fortunate family and social circumstances for which he can claim no credit."

18. Robert Nozick, *Anarchy, State, and Utopia* (New York: Basic Books, 1974), 39.

19. Rawls may protest because he views our moral character as acquired accidentally from family circumstances and such, so it is unclear whether for Rawls we can be implored to act justly since whether we do or not is not up to us. In short, is there room for genuine *moral* responsibility in Rawls' position? See Rawls, *A Theory of Justice,* 101–2.

20. See, for more on this, Tibor R. Machan, "Between Parents and Children," *The Journal of Social Philosophy* 3 (winter 1992), 16–22.

21. This is akin to how the choice to take up a profession implies the choice to carry out its crucial activities. One might think of the responsibility to think and act rationally as the content of an oath comparable to the Hippocratic oath taken by doctors. (For why implicit consent is a binding commitment to a principle of social life, see my *Individuals and Their Rights,* chapter 7.)

22. This holds even for those few who may have no means available to them to further their lives via the protection of their right to negative liberty—for example, the utterly incapacitated poor, since those who do have those capacities ought to strive to preserve the general, un-

exceptional conditions of human flourishing, meaning that they ought to maintain those rights that will help them to do so as human beings.

23. Communitarians object that individualism opposes community. To appreciate their confusion, see Douglas B. Rasmussen and Douglas J. Den Uyl, *Liberalism Defended: The Challenge of Post-Modernity* (London: Edward Elgar, 1997).

24. That the welfare state now and then does help some people is not a counterexample here. Some people crash in airplanes and live to write best-selling books about it. That does not mean that being in an airplane crash is per se good for your health. Moreover, the good done via the welfare state is demonstrably costly to those who were taxed so as to produce it; and that much of this cost ought not to be borne by them is a plausible thesis. That cost makes it more difficult to engage in the very act of flourishing, the conditions for which we want to ensure.

25. In recent times, the doctrine has been reshaped by such philosophers as James P. Sterba, Henry Shue, and legal scholars such as Stephen Holmes and Cass R. Sunstein.

26. Heather Gert, "Rights and Rights Violators: A New Approach to the Nature of Rights," *The Journal of Philosophy* 90 (1990): 688–94.

27. For a very pertinent discussion of Gert's point, unfortunately not discussed by her, see J. Roger Lee, "Choice and Harms," in Tibor R. Machan and M. B. Johnson, *Rights and Regulation* (San Francisco: Pacific Research Institute, 1983), 157–73.

28. Rasmussen and Den Uyl, *Liberty and Nature.*

29. Today it is communitarians who criticize rights theory most, including thinkers from both the right and the left. Their main objection is the alleged atomism of the individualist view involved in natural rights theory. They talk of how human beings belong to their communities and thus are wrongly regarded to be sovereign, autonomous persons. They claim that we have natural, enforceable obligations to others, to society or humanity, or to members of our neighborhood. The collective that is supreme keeps changing, but the point is always the same: The individual comes last. As Graham Greene puts it in *Loser Takes All* (Baltimore: Penguin Books, 1993), 15: "None of us has a right to forget anyone. Except ourselves." I discuss these and other objections to individualism in my *Classical Individualism* (London: Routledge, 1998).

30. Former Secretary of State James Baker declared, on a visit to the former Soviet colonies shortly after the fall of the Berlin Wall, that the case for freedom is that it works.

31. None should forget about slavery—but neither should one forget that that institution was abolished in part as a result of heeding the United States' first principles, not those of some alien political philosophy. Nor should we forget that the federal government of the United States has gradually lost sight of the principles of the Declaration of Independence on numerous fronts—not the least of which is foreign affairs, where it has slowly but surely become all too imperialistic not only for some good (e.g., the spreading of the idea of individual human rights) but also for evil (as in jingoistic military adventures, as chronicled in, for example, Warren Zimmermann, *First Great Triumph* [New York: Farrar, Straus, and Giroux, 2002]).

CHAPTER 1

1. Robert Kuttner, *Everything for Sale: The Virtues and Limits of Markets* (New York: Alfred A. Knopf, 1997).

2. For example, laws prohibiting interracial marriages, forbidding women to own property, and imposing special restrictions on voting for some qualify. Also, the abolition of any form of discrimination when it comes to obtaining government support, be this in the protection of one's rights, in a proper role for government, or in the distribution of benefits (public education), is not so proper a role for government.

3. Arguably, this is to underplay what many consider to be Hegel's notion of freedom. Hegel is known for regarding "true freedom" as identification of individual will with universal will (so that one is "free" even if one is enslaved in accord with a larger social purpose). As Copleston characterizes Hegel's idea:

And the unity of the particular will with the concept of the will in itself . . . is the good . . . which can be described as the "realization of freedom, the absolute final purpose of the world." The rational will as such is a man's true will, his will as a rational, free being.

See Frederick Copleston, S. J., *A History of Philosophy,* book 3, vol. 7, *Fichte to Nietzsche* (New York: Doubleday, 1985), 208.

So some might argue that the "freedom from obstacles" conception of freedom gives Hegel's notion a free pass, because Hegel's conception is not focused on the obstacles to individual goals as such but on the progress of the collective will/Spirit with which the individual must be aligned.

However, the conception of freedom that I have been attributing to the tradition in which Hegel plays a significant role is encompassed by Hegel's, even if it is not coextensive with it. For Hegel, though not for all who defend this conception of freedom as primary, the collective will/Spirit dictates what count as obstacles standing in the way of progress both for individuals and for humanity.

4. Copleston, *A History of Philosophy,* book 3, vol. 7, 131.

5. In the hands of a popularizer like Kuttner, the theory is a bit loose. Thus he criticizes a straw man version of market theory (akin to the game theory conception of man we have criticized) and says such things as "In a market, everything is potentially for sale. . . . One's person, one's vote, one's basic democratic rights do not belong on an auction block." As if all libertarians are advocates of slavery! He is more of a run-of-the-mill advocate of mixed-economy meddling, because markets don't "run themselves." See Robert Kuttner, "The Limits of Markets" (adapted from his book *Everything for Sale*), *The American Prospect* online (March–April 1997): www.prospect.org/archives/31/31kuttfs.html. It is actually democratic socialists who would place nearly everything on the ballot, so that people can vote away one's individual rights. See chapter 9 of this book for a fuller discussion of democracy and liberty.

CHAPTER 2

1. Calling this egoism "classical" also indicates its Aristotelian pedigree, which is also captured by the term "eudaimonist ethics."

2. For more on this, see Tibor R. Machan, *Classical Individualism* (London: Routledge, 1998); and Tibor R. Machan, *Generosity: Virtue in Civil Society* (Washington, D.C.: Cato Institute, 1998).

3. For more, see Ayn Rand, *The Virtue of Selfishness* (New York: New American Library, 1964). For a different approach, see David L. Norton, *Personal Destinies: A Philosophy of Ethical Individualism* (Princeton, N.J.: Princeton University Press, 1976).

4. James Rachels has rendered ethical egoism as follows: "Of course it is possible for people to act altruistically, and perhaps many people do act that way but there is no reason why they should do so. A person is under no obligation to do anything except what is in his

own interest." He notes that some "would point out that it is really not to my own advantage to set the fire—for, if I do that I may be caught and put into prison (unlike Gyges, I have no magic ring for protection)." He adds,

> Moreover, even if I could avoid being caught it is still to my advantage to respect the rights and interests of others, for it is to my advantage to live in a society in which people's rights and interests are respected. Only in such a society can I live a happy and secure life; so, in acting kindly toward others, I would merely be doing my part to create and maintain the sort of society which it is to my advantage to have. (14)

To this, Rachels replies

> But there is no reason for the egoist to think that merely because he will not honor the rules of the social game, decent society will collapse. For the vast majority of people are not egoists, and there is no reason to think that they will be converted by this example—especially if he is discrete and does not unduly flaunt his style of life. What this line of reasoning shows is not that the egoist himself must act benevolently, but that he must encourage others to do so. (14)

In James Rachels, *The Elements of Moral Philosophy,* 2nd ed. (New York: McGraw-Hill, 1993).

Classical egoism, however, is based on human nature, on what is proper to a human individual by virtue of his or her essential or fundamental attributes. The proper way for one to act is constitutive of that individual's human good, not merely an optional instrument. In contrast, Rachels characterizes ethical egoism as nothing but a Machiavellian system of strategies by which individuals pursue whatever they like, never mind what is objectively good for them.

It is curious that many moral philosophers do not appreciate that the best life to be lived by anyone is that life which makes a human being excellent. It is in one's own interest, then, to be moral since that is how one can be the best one can be.

CHAPTER 3

1. It is worth noting here that the very idea of "the nature of X" is highly disputed by philosophers. Among them, for example, Daniel

C. Dennett, the 2001 president of the American Philosophical Association, rejects it, as does Richard Rorty, another very prominent member of the profession of academic philosophers. But the main reason is that in one influential tradition, founded in the thought of Plato, the nature of something is seen as separate from it—say, the nature of a chair stands apart from chairs—and is perfect, timeless, etc. Since this couldn't be known by temporal human beings, it was eventually dismissed as an untenable idea. For more on this, see Tibor R. Machan, "Liberalism and Atomistic Individualism," *Journal of Value Inquiry* 34 (September 2000): 227–47.

CHAPTER 5

1. See, however, John Kekes, "'Ought Implies Can' and Kinds of Morality," *Philosophical Quarterly* 34 (1984): 460–67; John Kekes, *Facing Evil* (Princeton, N.J.: Princeton University Press, 1991); as well as John Kekes, "Freedom," *Pacific Philosophical Quarterly* 61 (1980): 368–85. See also, Tibor R. Machan, "Applied Ethics and Free Will," *Journal of Applied Philosophy* 10 (1993): 59–72.

2. That is, were, say, utilitarianism the right ethical theory, the ethics of parenting would have to fully conform to it.

3. Some actually deny that this is necessary, specifically in discussions of military ethics. See Nicholas Fotion and Gerard Elfstrom, *Military Ethics: Guidelines for Peace and War* (Boston: Routledge & Kegan Paul, 1986); and Nicholas G. Fotion, *Military Ethics: Looking Toward the Future* (Stanford, Calif.: Hoover Institution Press, Stanford University, 1990). Fotion, especially, rejects the idea that military ethics requires some sort of systematic foundation.

4. See Tibor R. Machan, "Ethics and Its Uses," in Tibor R. Machan, ed., *Commerce and Morality* (Lanham, Md.: Rowman & Littlefield, 1988); and Machan, "Applied Ethics and Free Will."

CHAPTER 6

1. Adam Smith, *The Wealth of Nations* (New York: Modern Library, 1927), 726.

2. Reprinted in slightly revised form as "Capitalism, Socialism, and Nihilism," *The Public Interest,* no. 31 (spring 1973): 3–16. Kristol

works within the tradition or school that aligns itself with Leo Strauss' conception of the Greek ideas and ideals. The idea of a common good that is the natural purpose of a human community has a central role with this political tradition, although the specific virtues that people must cultivate for proper realization of that ideal are rarely discussed by members of this school.

3. Harry Browne, *How I Found Freedom in an Unfree World* (New York: Macmillan, 1973), especially the chapter on "The Morality Trap."

4. For a discussion of the place and function of morality in human life, see Eric Mack, "How to Derive Egoism," *The Personalist* (autumn 1971): 735–43.

5. Roger W. Sperry, "Mind, Brain and Humanistic Values," in John I. Platt, ed., *New Views on the Nature of Man* (Chicago: University of Chicago Press, 1965); Robert Efron, "Biology without Consciousness—and Its Consequences," *Perspectives in Biology and Medicine* (autumn 1967): 9–36; Isidor Chein, *The Science of Behavior and the Image of Man* (New York: Basic Books, 1972); and Tibor R. Machan, *The Pseudo-Science of B. F. Skinner* (New Rochelle, N.Y.: Arlington House, 1974).

6. Even when scientists argued this case, they did not do so by reference to their scientific discoveries but by way of invalid extrapolation—cf. B. F. Skinner, *Beyond Freedom and Dignity* (New York: Knopf, 1970); and, much earlier, Thomas Hobbes, David Hume, and other determinists also proceeded in this manner.

7. See my discussion of why this is so in Machan, *The Pseudo-Science*; and in Tibor R. Machan, "Kuhn, Impossibility Proof and the Moral Element in Scientific Explanations," *Theory and Decision* 4 (1974): 355–74.

8. For a clear discussion see Chein, *The Science of Behavior*; and A. R. Louch, *Explanation and Human Action* (Berkeley: University of California Press, 1966).

9. Sperry, "Mind, Brain"; Chein, *The Science of Behavior*; and Nathaniel Branden, *The Psychology of Self-Esteem* (Los Angeles: Nash, 1968). For a full discussion of the issue, see Tibor R. Machan, *Initiative—Human Agency and Society* (Stanford, Calif.: Hoover Institution Press, 2000).

10. There are those, of course, who offer such a defense. See Ayn Rand, *The Virtue of Selfishness* (New York: Signet, 1964); Ayn Rand, *Capitalism: The Unknown Ideal* (New York: Signet, 1966); and H. B. Acton, *The Morals of Markets* (London: Longman, 1971).

11. This is not true of intellectuals who fall outside the scope of the present discussion, yet even strict Marxists must hold, with Marx, that capitalism is for the present the most efficient economic arrangement for human beings.

12. The books written by "Nader's Raiders" in support of these contentions include James M. Fallows, *The Water Lords* (New York: Grossman Publishers, 1971); Mark J. Green, *Closed Enterprise System* (New York: Grossman Publishers, 1972); and John C. Esposito and Larry J. Silverman, *Vanishing Air* (New York: Grossman Publishers, 1970). Nader's most explicit economic discussion appeared in Ralph Nader, "A Citizen's Guide to the American Economy," *The New York Review of Books,* September 2, 1971. This last piece contains all the standard myths about the waste of advertising, exploitative profits, and the like, but gains its plausibility in view of the considerable validity of Nader's charges concerning collusion between big business and the regulatory agencies of the federal and state governments.

13. Since theoretical cases are produced by human beings, it is possible to offer a moral criticism of them—for example, that they are dishonest, sloppy, and self-contradictory.

14. It is the lack of concern for these that Kristol laments within the classical liberal tradition. As a counter to this charge with reference to earlier classical liberals, see Ralph Raico, "The Fusionists on Liberalism and Tradition," *New Individualist Review* 3, no. 3 (1964): 29–36.

15. Kristol, "Capitalism, Socialism," 15–16.

16. For a clear statement of this point, see the interview with Yale Brozen, *Reason* 5, no. 8 (December 1973): 4–12.

17. That is, those we are discussing, although even among members of the Chicago School there exist differences of deemphasis of ethics.

18. David Friedman, *The Machinery of Freedom* (New York: Harper & Row, 1973), 223. Armen Alchian and Harold Demsetz have expressed their skepticism to me in person and have included their ideas to this effect in public lectures, for example, at the property rights conferences sponsored by the Institute for Humane Studies in Claremont, California (1969), and Rockford, Illinois (1970).

19. From the point of view of methodology—in other words, what is construed to be the sort of evidence and the type of theory that may be admitted within economics as such—almost all of those at Chicago are empiricists (including, of course, their students). The

"empiricist" label does not serve to refer to other value-free oriented economists who support the free market—for example, Ludwig von Mises and F. A. Hayek.

20. Acton, *The Morals of Markets,* 101.

21. On the relationship between the free expression of ideas, including artistic and political ones, and the free market, see Ayn Rand's essay, "Censorship: Local and Express," in Ayn Rand, *Philosophy: Who Needs It* (Indianapolis: The Bobbs-Merrill Co., 1982), 211–30.

22. *Lynch v. Household Finance Corp.,* 31 L. Ed. 2d 424 (1972).

23. Personal communication, November 1, 1973.

24. Quoted in Norval Morris and Gordon Hawkins, *The Honest Politician's Guide to Crime Control* (Chicago: University of Chicago Press, 1970), 84.

25. Obviously the subjectivist theory of ethics is not confined to supporters of Friedman's brand of economics, but among those supporting the free market this last group is most prominent.

26. There are many personal vices and evils. People can engage in them alone or in voluntary cooperation, but their witness would violate others' moral agency—their very capacity for good and evil—by making efforts at improving them in ways other than persuasive. "I think," said Pericles, "that everything which someone, without using persuasion, forces another to do, whether by decree or not, is force, not law." Quoted in Xenophon, *Memorabilia,* 1, 2, 4–46.

27. Kristol, "Capitalism, Socialism," 15–16.

28. Kristol, "Capitalism, Socialism," 16.

29. Leo Strauss, *Natural Right and History* (Chicago: University of Chicago Press, 1952).

30. Kristol is one of those who have expressed high regard for Leo Strauss' political thought and have tried to make it influential in public affairs.

31. Strauss, *Natural Right and History,* 131.

CHAPTER 7

1. Consider Holmes's dissent in the famous case of *Lochner v. New York* (1905)—in which the justice archly noted that the Fourteenth Amendment "does not enact Mr. Herbert Spencer's *Social Statics*"—an opinion that would have more influence than that of the majority. See www.lectlaw.com/files/case37.htm.

CHAPTER 8

1. See, for example, Randy Barnett, *The Structure of Liberty* (London: Oxford University Press, 1998).

2. Although the right to own property may be unalienable, what one owns is not, and it may be traded, given away, and even destroyed—as Karl Marx was so eager to point out in his essay, "On The Jewish Question," in Karl Marx, *Selected Writings,* ed. D. McLellan (London: Oxford University Press, 1977).

3. Charles Taylor, *Philosophy and the Human Sciences* (London: Cambridge University Press, 1985), 188.

4. The concept "belong" can be used to refer to membership as well as to being a part of something. Membership in human communities embarking on various purposes can be voluntary, but "being a part of" something is ontologically pregnant—one is part of something sometimes whether one likes it or not. By "belong," Taylor seems clearly to mean "being part of," so that one can be compelled to adhere to the purpose at hand.

5. Marx, *Selected Writings,* 126.

6. Karl Marx, *Grundrisse,* trans. D. McLellan (New York: Harper Torchbooks, 1971), 39.

7. I develop much of this throughout Tibor R. Machan, *Classical Individualism: The Supreme Importance of Each Human Being* (London: Routledge, 1998), especially in chapter 13, "Individualism and Political Dialogue." Any kind of professional, including scholarly and intellectual, malpractice alleged in the course of political or other disputes implicitly assigns responsibility with the interlocutors, blaming or commending them for what they ought to or ought not to have done or said.

8. Exceptions are individuals who are crucially incapacitated. Political theory and law are not devices for dealing with exceptions, however.

9. For more on this, see Edward Pols, *Acts of Our Being* (Boston: University of Massachusetts Press, 1982); and Tibor R. Machan, *Initiative: Human Agency and Society* (Stanford, Calif.: Hoover Institution Press, 2000).

10. This is what public choice theory, within contemporary political economy, has helped identify. See, however, Harold Kincaid, *Philosophical Foundations of the Social Sciences: Analyzing Controversies in Social Research* (London: Cambridge University Press,

1996), in which the author argues that the individualist stance in modern economics is mistaken and that we ought to deploy a more holistic approach. Kincaid and many other critics of what they dub "liberal individualism" claim that individualism is atomistic. Although some individualists may fit this description, certainly not all of them do. Nor is that the only version of individualism that gives rise to liberal politics. Good cases in point include John Locke, among the early liberals; and Ayn Rand, Eric Mack, Douglas B. Rasmussen, Douglas J. Den Uyl, Fred D. Miller, Jr., and the late David L. Norton, among many others, in our own age.

11. Economists use Crusoe on the island to abstract away from social complications as they explain elementary economic truths, the nature of marginal utility, the implications of resource scarcity, etc. Then they add Friday to the story and eventually other people. This could be an example of how atomism has sometimes unjustifiably been imputed to economic reasoning by antagonists who want something to seize upon. Even if individualist writers have sometimes given cause for the atomistic perception, it is also true that collectivist writers have seen the bogeyman of atomism where it is not implied.

12. In Eduard Zeller, *Aristotle and the Earlier Peripatetics*, trans. B. F. C. Costelloe and J. H. Muirhead (London: Oxford University Press, 1897), Zeller wrote:

> To [Aristotle] the Individual is the primary reality, and has the first claim to recognition. In his metaphysics individual things are regarded, not as the mere shadows of the idea, but as independent realities; universal conceptions not as independent substances but as the expression for the common peculiarity of a number of individuals. Similarly in his moral philosophy he transfers the ultimate end of human action and social institutions from the State to the individual, and looks for its attainment in his free self-development. The highest aim of the State consists in the happiness of its citizens. (224–26)

This idea is developed further in Fred D. Miller, Jr., *Nature, Justice, and Rights in Aristotle's Politics* (Oxford: Clarendon Press, 1995). The difference between the atomistic and classical type of individualism is discussed in Tibor R. Machan, *Capitalism and Individualism: Reframing the Argument for the Free Society* (New York: St. Martin's Press, 1990).

13. A very important beginning had been made on this line of analysis by the fourteenth-century English philosopher William of Ockham, who regarded property rights as securing "the power of rights reason," that is, a sphere of personal jurisdiction that made reasoning about what one ought to do possible. This was elaborated in John Locke's idea that one has the right to one's person and estate, something that, if protected, makes choice among other persons possible. An even greater advance on the precise identification of the nature of private property had been made in James Sadowsky, "Private Property and Collective Ownership," in Tibor R. Machan, ed., *The Libertarian Alternative* (Chicago: Nelson Hall, 1974). Karl Marx, too, got it nearly right when he wrote that "the right of man to property is the right to enjoy his possessions and dispose of the same arbitrarily without regard for other men, independently, from society, the right of selfishness." Karl Marx, "On the Jewish Question," in Robert C. Tucker, ed., *The Marx-Engels Reader* (New York: W. W. Norton, 1978), 26. But Marx's warped view of human nature prompted him to consider only the most wasteful and pointless way in which the right to private property might be exercised.

14. Douglas B. Rasmussen and Douglas J. Den Uyl, *Liberty and Nature* (Chicago, Ill.: Open Court Publishing Co., 1990).

15. For more on this, see Tibor R. Machan, "The Normative Basis of Economic Science," *Economic Affairs* 18 (June 1998): 43–46.

16. Augustine, *Confessions,* book 10, chapter 17, 8ff.

17. Victor Hugo, *La preface de Cromwell,* ed. Maurice A. Souriau (Geneva: Slatkine Reprints, 1973).

18. Adam Smith, *The Wealth of Nations* (Indianapolis, Ind.: Liberty Classics, 1994), 26–27. But see also Smith's observation, in this very same work, lamenting the same point at issue here, quoted on page 73 herein.

CHAPTER 9

1. "Nominal" in this sense means "common meaning in name only."

2. Among those on the Left, the work of Benjamin Barker, *Strong Democracy* (Berkeley: University of California Press, 1990), stands out as a sustained argument for the priority of democracy over other con-

siderations. Others, too, have stressed this, among them Richard Rorty and Jurgen Habermas.

3. The nature of tacit consent is complicated, admittedly, but clearly such consent exists—for example, when I tacitly consent to your using my bathroom upon having invited you to my house for dinner. In social-political affairs, what amounts to implicit or tacit consent can be complicated, of course, but I shall not dwell on the matter here. I have done this in my book *Individuals and Their Rights* (LaSalle, Ill.: Open Court Publishing Co., 1989), chapter 7, "Individualism and Political Authority."

4. This is duplicity. If Republicans, for example, elect to cut federal programs that leave open the possibility that some states will not spend money on poor children's lunches, that is supposed to be mean-minded, cruel, and morally insidious according to their critics, including many Democrats. But if Democrats decide to increase taxes for various programs that intrude on the liberty of various citizens, this isn't wrong and is often defended by noting that this is just the way democracy works, so all those suffering the adverse consequences have no reason to complain. We did it to ourselves, so we have no right to fuss.

5. This is one basic flaw of legal positivism in the United States, as propounded by Robert Bork: It endorses, as the proper approach to making law, the democratic (or some other preferred law-making) process because it expresses the will of the people or the sovereign, as opposed to judicial review, which is illegitimately prescriptive. Yet where does legal positivism make room for the defense of its prescriptions?

6. Robert Nozick, *The Examined Life* (New York: Simon and Schuster, 1989), 286–87.

7. Henry Hazlitt, from "Three Blessings in One," an address before the Chamber of Commerce of the United States in Washington, D.C., April 30, 1962. It appeared in *The Freeman* (August 1962).

CHAPTER 13

1. See, in this connection, Lt. Colonel Charles J. Dunlop, Jr., "The Origins of the American Military Coup of 2012," *Parameters: The United States Army War College Quarterly* (winter 1992–1993): 2–20.

Dunlop argues that deploying the military for extraneous, nondefensive purposes is likely to convince military leaders and enthusiasts that they, not civilians, ought to be governing the country.

CHAPTER 14

1. For a detailed discussion of this understanding of rights, see the essays in Tibor R. Machan, *Individual Rights Reconsidered* (Stanford, Calif.: Hoover Institution Press, 2001), especially the one by Tom G. Palmer.

2. The idea of positive rights emerged in full force in the writings of such political philosophers as T. H. Green, Bernard Bosanquet, and, more recently, Henry Shue, James P. Sterba, and others.

3. See Henry Shue, *Basic Rights* (Princeton, N.J.: Princeton University Press, 1970); and Stephen Holmes and Cass R. Sunstein, *The Cost of Rights: Why Liberty Depends on Taxes* (New York: W. W. Norton, 1999), 21.

4. See Dunlop "The Origins of the American Military Coup of 2012," 2–20. For more on this, see Dana Priest, *The Mission: Waging War and Keeping Peace with America's Military* (New York: W.W. Norton, 2003).

CHAPTER 15

1. If one were to think that only left-wing ideologues invoke political correctness, this is a clear example of how those on the right do so as well. Using *unborn child* emotionally loads the debate in ways that *fetus* does not—the colloquial usage leaves open whether fetuses are actual or potential human beings. (*Foetus* or fetus means "coming into being" in reference to animals and humans. See *The Compact Edition of the Oxford English Dictionary,* 1039.) Of course, all sides to a controversy attempt to slant language to serve their goals, but it becomes political correctness when others are being pressured to accept this language, especially in the major media.

2. St. Thomas Aquinas discussed the process of human generation in four places: In 2 Sent., d.18, q.2, aa.1,3; *Summa Contra Gentiles* 2, cc. 86–89; *De Potentia Dei*, q.3, aa.9–12; and ST 1a, q.118. See an analysis of this by Taylor (1981). For a paper that relates Thomas'

teaching to modern embryology, see Ford (1989), 19–64. See also Wallace (1995); I borrow Wallace's reference to Aquinas' discussion of quickening and such without having verified them.

For one relevant passage, see Thomas Aquinas, *De Potentia Dei*, q.3, a.12, which reads as follows:

> Secundum quod Philosophus probat in XV De animalibus, semen non deciditur ab eo quod fuit actu pars, sed quod fuit superfluum ultimae digestionis; quod nondum erat ultima assimilatione assimilatum. Nulla autem corporis pars est actu per animam perfecta, nisi sit ultima assimilatione assimilata; unde semen ante decisionem nondum erat perfectum per animam, ita quod anima esset forma eius; erat tamen ibi aliqua virtus, secundum quam iam per actionem animae erat alteratum et deductum ad dispositionem propinquam ultimae assimilationi; unde et postquam decisum est, non est ibi anima, sed aliqua virtus animae. (quoted in Wallace, 1995: 407)

> As the philosopher proves in *On Animals* XV [=Of the *Generation of Animals* I, 18 and 19], seed is not separated from that of which it was actually a part, but from what was superfluous in what had been digested, which was not yet completely assimilated. No part of the body is actually perfected by soul unless it is completely assimilated, which is why semen prior to emission was not yet perfected by soul in such wise that soul would be its form, but there was in it some power thanks to which by the action of the soul it was altered and led to a disposition close to ultimate assimilation, hence after emission there is not soul in it but rather some power [effect] of the soul. (Trans. Ralph McInerny)

3. What contemporary Roman Catholics say is this: "Human life must be respected and protected absolutely from the moment of conception. From the first moment of his existence, a human being must be recognized as having the rights of a person—among which is the inviolable right of every innocent being to life." *Catechism of the Catholic Church* (Washington, D.C.: United States Catholic Conference, 1994), para. 2270; available at www.catholic-forum.com luxveritatis/donumsanctum/abortion.htm.

Now this claim is ambiguous for several reasons and begs the question to boot. "Every innocent being" may mean all living beings capable of sinning but not having sinned, or it could include all living beings without sin, including animals other than human beings. However, there is another problem with this view as part of Roman Catholic doctrine: If at birth we are sinful—that is, are possessed of *original sin*—and need to be baptized so as to be cleansed of our original sin(s), then from conception until baptism we are not "innocent beings." A Roman Catholic says,

> Abortion is wrong because it is an act that runs counter to natural, eternal, and divine law. That is, abortion is wrong for the same reason many sins are wrong. Abortion is murder, which Aquinas rules to be one of those sins that cannot be justified by any means or circumstances. (*Catechism of the Catholic Church,* para. 2270)

Aquinas cannot be interpreted as simply holding that all abortions are murder, granting though, as we must, that he did hold that murder is a sin of the highest order. Most pro-choice advocates agree with him and with pro-life advocates on that. The dispute centers around whether in early pregnancy the woman carries a human being or, instead, a human fetus (and, thus, only a potential human being).

CHAPTER 16

1. Actually, this kind of fair treatment is due to anyone who signs up for a service provided to a group, as when teachers are obliged to address the needs of all the students in their class or coaches to train all those on a team.

Government owes the protection of basic rights to all citizens, not because, as some have argued, it created these rights or because of some absolute, basic egalitarian principle but because all of us signed up for the service, as it were, and thus got it promised to us, in effect. See, for an opposite view, Henry Shue, *Basic Rights* (Princeton, N.J.: Princeton University Press, 1980); and Stephen Holmes and Cass R. Sunstein, *The Cost of Rights: Why Liberty Depends on Taxes* (New York: W. W. Norton, 1999). But see also Tibor R. Machan, "The Perils of Positive Rights," *Ideas on Liberty* 51 (April 2001): 49–52; Tibor R. Machan, "Moral Myths and Basic Positive Rights," *Tulane Studies in Philosophy* 33 (1985): 35–41; and Tibor R. Machan, "The Non-Existence of Welfare Rights," in Lawrence Hinman, ed., *Contemporary Moral Issues* (Upper Saddle River, N.J.: Prentice Hall, 1996).

2. Of course, if I announce that my offer of a service or good is available *to all potential purchasers,* I may be liable if I then impose, capriciously, an unannounced standard of selection after the fact. If no

disclosure of special criteria is made in such a context, it is reasonable to expect that none will be applied. Remedies would then be available in a just system of laws.

3. Of course, banning of association that involves violating the rights of others would still be prohibited, because the entailed rights violation is per se prohibited, no matter what form the violation takes. Arguably, membership in a criminal gang could then be illegal, as might be membership in the KKK or any other organizations that are known to be embarking on rights-violating conduct.

Of course, within a developed legal system many of these matters are dealt with in complicated, technical ways. The purpose here is to lay out some of the broad principles of a free and just society, not to detail the application of those principles within the context of a complex social life.

4. Richard A. Epstein, *Forbidden Grounds: The Case against Employment Discrimination Laws* (Cambridge, Mass.: Harvard University Press, 1992).

5. Jim Sleeper makes this point in *Liberal Racism* (New York: Viking, 1997).

6. For more on this, see Shelby Steele, *A Dream Deferred* (New York: HarperCollins Publishers, 1998).

EPILOGUE

1. Ludwig von Mises, *Liberalism: In the Classical Tradition,* trans. Ralph Raico (Irvington-on-Hudson, N.Y.: Foundation for Economic Education, 1985), 193.

2. Blaise Pascal, quoted in *The Week,* July 27, 2002, 17.

INDEX

abortion, 177
Acton, H.B., 81, 225n10
Adams, John Q., 108
advertising, 207
affirmative action, 189-191
Alchien, Armen, 226n18
altruism, 66, 80
Aquinas, Thomas, 181, 233n2
Aristotle, 31, 107, 112, 125, 179, 182, 212
autonomy, 13, 85

Baker, James, 220n30
Barker, Benjamin, 231n2
Barnett, Randy, 228n1
Bastiat, 126
Beethoven, 48
Boaz, David, 94
Bork, Robert, 131, 231n5
Bosanquet, Bernard, 232n2
Bright, 126
Brimelow, Peter, 62
Browne, Harry, 225n3
Brozen, Yale, 76, 226n16
Buchanan, Patrick, 59,62
Bukovsky, Vladimir, 51
Butler, Bishop, 31
Bush, George W., 150

capitalism , free markets: class warfare
    and, 141-143; consequentialist
    defense of, 45-46; criticism of, 122;
    defintion of, 42; disdain for, 126;
    hatred of, 39-40; individualism
    inherent in, 40; moral agency
    necessary for, 51-52; moral choice
    and, 44; moral defense of, 46, 76;
    property rights implied in, 42
Chein, Isidor, 225n5, 225n8
Chicago School, 76, 84-87, 225n17
civil rights, 189
Clinton, William J., President, 94
Cobden, 126
commons, tragedy of the, 50, 119, 137
communitarianism, 37-39, 103
Copleston, Frederick, S.J., 221n3
Costelloe, B.F.C., 229n12

democracy: as a just process, 129;
    fascism resulting from, 53;
    immigration and, 60; individualism
    a part of, 19-20; natural rights
    basis of, 130-134; positive rights
    issuing from, 173
Demsetz, Harold,, 226n18
Den Uyl, Douglas, 22, 120, 218n7,
    219n14, 220n23

ABOUT THE AUTHOR

Tibor R. Machan teaches at the Argyros School of Business and Economics, Chapman University, Orange, California, and is a research fellow at the Hoover Institution, Stanford University, California. He advises Freedom Communications, Inc., a family-owned media company, on public policy issues. Machan, who earned a Ph.D. in philosophy at University of California Santa Barbara, has written over twenty books and edited another twenty. He was smuggled out of Hungary in 1953, came to the United States three years later, and served in the U.S. Air Force before undertaking his formal education. He lives in Silverado, in southern California. You can visit his website at www.TiborMachan.com.